**Marisol
Portrait
Sculpture**

Magical Mixtures:
Marisol
Portrait
Sculpture

Nancy Grove

Published by the Smithsonian
Institution Press
for the National Portrait Gallery
Washington, D.C.

**An exhibition at the
National Portrait Gallery
April 5 to August 11, 1991**

Library of Congress
Cataloging-in-Publication Data
Grove, Nancy.
    Magical mixtures—Marisol portrait
sculpture / Nancy Grove.
            p. cm.
    ''An exhibition at the National Portrait
Gallery, April 5 to August 11, 1991''—T.p.
verso.
    Includes bibliographical references (p.)
and index.
    ISBN 1-56098-042-7
    1. Marisol, 1930–   —Exhibitions.
I. Marisol, 1930– . II. National Portrait
Gallery (Smithsonian Institution) III. Title.
NB439.M3A4 1991
709'.2— dc20   90-50892

Cover illustration
Self-portrait by Marisol
Mixed media, 110.5 cm. (43½ in),
1961–1962
Museum of Contemporary Art; promised
gift of Joseph and Jory Shapiro

Contents

Foreword

Except for a few independent souls who steadfastly have refused to honor the vanity of their subjects or the aesthetic timidity of patrons, portraiture in our age has been left, for the most part, to painters and sculptors with a decidedly conventional approach to their craft. Given the fact that those who make portraits for a living must satisfy not only sitters and their families but also the corporations, government officials, and others who commission likenesses, it is hardly surprising that these artists have been reluctant to push their art to the limits of the avant-garde.

With the notable exception of portraits of artists, writers, and composers, most of the work by contemporary artists acquired by the National Portrait Gallery, or shown in its special exhibitions, has tended to reflect this conservative aesthetic, leading some to the conclusion that there is an unbridgeable gulf between imaginative art and portraiture. A look at any of the remarkable three-dimensional portraits produced by Marisol over the past thirty years will immediately correct this misapprehension.

Marisol has created a series of perfectly recognizable images that exist in a context entirely of her own creation. Her people emerge from blocks of polished or painted wood, or from a construction of "found" objects, and somehow she manages to satirize a physical characteristic, to comment upon the way a subject presents himself or herself to the world, or to suggest an affectionate relationship. Although Marisol's style is manifestly of the twentieth century, her incorporation of objects that relate to the subject's life or work is reminiscent of the work of much older artists, and though her work is at home in museums and art galleries, her use and combination of materials and textures suggest that she has been enchanted by the folk artists of the three continents on which she has worked.

Individual examples of Marisol's portraits have been shown on many occasions here at the National Portrait Gallery, but this is the first time that any museum has been able to assemble an exhibition devoted to her portraiture in depth. We are indebted to Nancy Grove for proposing the idea and for executing it so deftly, and we are grateful to the many lenders to the exhibition who have allowed us to share these fascinating objects with our public. Most of all, we are thankful to Marisol for creating what she has, for assisting Ms. Grove and our staff in their work, and for allowing us to bring this remarkable body of work together.

Alan Fern
Director
National Portrait Gallery

Acknowledgments

First and foremost, I would like to thank Marisol for her cooperation throughout the planning of this exhibition. She took time out of a busy work schedule to look through old photographs, to give me her thoughts on what pieces might be appropriate for the show, and to comment on the ideas and information in the catalogue entries. It has been an honor and a pleasure to work with her.

Thanks must also go to the staff of the Sidney Janis Gallery, especially Jeffrey Figley. He has been most generous with his time and help, cheerfully coping with innumerable urgent requests for photographs and information. Many thanks are due as well to Mrs. Edwin A. Bergman and Mr. and Mrs. Brooks Barron, who responded promptly and graciously to my inquiries about their Marisols.

Valuable help was also provided by Judith Du Pres of the Abrams Family Collection; Nelly Bly Cogan, development coordinator of the Miami University Art Museum; and Michelle Matlack of the Museum of Modern Art.

Many people at the National Portrait Gallery have contributed in important ways to this exhibition. Director Alan Fern's insightful comments improved the catalogue essay substantially. This publication benefited greatly from the expert, author-friendly editing of Frances Stevenson and Dru Dowdy. Vandy Cook and Claire Kelly tracked down hard-to-find photographs and information with great persistence. Nello Marconi and Al Elkins's exhibition design, as always, provided an interesting and appropriate setting for the sculptures.

My greatest thanks, however, must go to Curator of Exhibitions Beverly J. Cox, whose enthusiasm and support have been crucial to the realization of this show. It wouldn't and couldn't have happened without her, and I am most grateful.

Nancy Grove
Brooklyn, New York

Marisol
Portrait
Sculpture

7

Lenders to the Exhibition

Mr. and Mrs. Brooks Barron

Mrs. Edwin A. Bergman

Colorado Springs Fine Arts
Center, Colorado

Hood Museum of Art,
Dartmouth College,
Hanover, New Hampshire

Sidney Janis Gallery,
New York, New York

Marisol

Miami University Art
Museum, Oxford, Ohio

Museum of Contemporary Art,
Chicago, Illinois

The Museum of Modern Art,
New York, New York

National Museum of
American Art, Smithsonian
Institution, Washington, D.C.

National Portrait Gallery,
Smithsonian Institution,
Washington, D.C.

Rose Art Museum, Brandeis
University, Waltham,
Massachusetts

Joseph D. and Janet M. Shein

A Point of View: The Portraits of Marisol

In the 1929 film *Un Chien Andalou,* made by Spanish Surrealists Luis Buñuel and Salvador Dali, a young woman carefully arranges a man's collar, cuffs, and other accessories on a bed, then sits down and stares at them until the man himself materializes into the clothing. Looking at a portrait by the Venezuelan-American sculptor Marisol is like that. You see a collection of wooden boxes, carved and painted surfaces, plaster casts, objects, and pieces of clothing; as you study this assembly, a personality magically emerges. Given her power to conjure individuals from imaginative conjunctions of unlikely materials, it is surprising that Marisol is not better known as a portraitist, especially as she has created more than forty sculptures of people in the fields of art, entertainment, and politics, as well as many self-portraits.

Indeed, when considered in the context of her work as a whole, it is clear that the portrait has been one of Marisol's main ways of expressing herself since the early 1960s. The special nature of her portraiture is equally clear: no one sits for Marisol, who prefers to reconstruct her subjects from memory, photographs, and objects. Her contribution to the history of the portrait is her invention of a way of making likenesses that does not depend on patronage or, as in Warhol's work, on the literal appropriation of media images. She always has a point of view, and she can assemble highly personal objects from basic public facts.

Marisol is better known for multifigure ensembles that combine blocky materials, media images, and found objects in witty evocations of modern society. Now, however, other aspects of her work are beginning to be noticed. Her autobiographical pieces can be reevaluated in relation to the self-involved art of the 1970s and 1980s; her images of role-playing men and women have begun to be considered in the light of their implied critique of 1960s sexism, and she herself is appreciated as "the only woman artist to have emerged during the Pop movement and survived."[1] Indeed, her work is an example of steady achievement and strong personal evolution without excessive or destructive audacity. As sculptor George Segal has put it: "Marisol's art has always had wit, but she's dead serious. She brings a complexity to her work, which has a sobering gravity. She's an original."[2]

She once said: "Whatever the artist makes is always a kind of self-portrait."[3] In Marisol's work there is a unique, ongoing dialogue between the self and society that depended, in the 1960s, upon her ability to identify with people from every facet and level of society and, at the same time, to use her own face and body as a "found object." The intense social explorations of the 1960s were followed by a period of introspection in the 1970s, and in her recent work she has again turned away from self-portraiture to cast an increasingly expressive eye on revered elders and pressing world problems. The importance of Marisol's art lies in the ways it broadens traditional definitions of sculpture while providing a wry running commentary on the state of society and the self.

"Aztec out of Lipchitz": Early Life and Work

Born in Paris in 1930 to Venezuelans Gustavo and Josefina Hernandez Escobar, Marisol (who has been known by that single name—"sea and sun" in Spanish—since the 1950s) spent her first years traveling in Europe with her family, including her brother Gustavo, now an economist. When she was five, the family began to commute between Caracas and the United States; after her mother died in 1941, she was sent to boarding school for a time. It was then that she acquired the habit of silence that would be much commented on in the gregarious 1960s: "When I was 11, I decided never to talk again. I didn't want to sound the way other people did. I really didn't talk for years except for what was absolutely necessary in school and on the street. They used to think I was crazy."[4] During World War II the family remained in Caracas, but in 1946 her father, who was supportive of her ambition to be an artist, took her to Los Angeles, where she attended the Westwood School for Girls and enrolled in night classes in painting with Howard Warshaw at the Jepson School. In 1949 she went to Paris to study at the École des Beaux-Arts, but left after a year, declaring, "It was like nothing. They wanted me to paint like Bonnard."[5] She then went to New York and began to take painting classes with Yasuo Kuniyoshi at the Art Students League. However, she soon transferred to Hans Hofmann's painting school, where she studied from 1951 to 1954. She also took classes at the New School for Social Research. Later she would say that Hofmann was the only teacher from whom she learned anything.[6] He had taught in Munich from 1915 until 1932, when he settled permanently in the United States. His New York school opened in 1933 and operated until his death in 1966. Hofmann's ideas about the spiritual and expressive nature of art may have influenced his young student. Although he taught painting, he had published his thoughts on sculpture in a 1948 essay which said, in part, "Sculpture deals with basic forms. The basic forms are: cubes, cones, spheres, and pyramids. Every subject has a characteristic basic form. These forms can be intensified by opposing them to other basic forms."[7] The principle of opposition of forms and forces, or "push-pull," was important to Hofmann's colorful, dynamic abstractions. In 1963 an article about Marisol's sculpture would note: "Three dimensions sink into two; two grow into three in a sort of Marisol version of Hans Hofmann's theory of push-and-pull."[8]

In 1950, the year Marisol came to New York, Abstract Expressionism was the established style. Painters such as Hofmann, Jackson Pollock, Robert Motherwell, Willem de Kooning, Franz Kline, and Mark Rothko were known for their lyrical, deeply felt abstractions. They met and exchanged ideas at the Cedar Bar or at Friday

night meetings of the Artists Club on Eighth Street in Greenwich Village. Artists were becoming increasingly articulate and interested in educating the art world about modern art. In 1950, for example, a group of painters called the "Irascibles" challenged the figurative bias of a juried exhibition of American painting at the Metropolitan Museum of Art.[9] Supported by sculptors David Smith, Theodore Roszak, Herbert Ferber, David Hare, Ibram Lassaw, and Seymour Lipton, the Irascibles protested the museum's policies and boycotted the competition. When the museum held a similar exhibition of American sculpture in 1951, few abstract sculptors acted as jurors or were included in it.

In response to the museum controversies, sixty-one abstract artists organized their own "Ninth Street Show" in 1951; artist-run exhibitions and galleries quickly proliferated. Many of the artists involved were abstractionists, but not all. One of the founding members of the artist-run Tanager Gallery, for example, was figurative sculptor William King, who was interested in the work of early twentieth-century émigré sculptor Elie Nadelman and, like Nadelman, in American folk art. King worked in wood, clay, and other materials, "creating pseudo-primitive, subtly humorous and narrative social commentaries. . . . His essential concern with attitudes and poses to explore conventional social stereotypes would become important for the sixties as further developed by Marisol, Ernest Trova and George Segal."[10] Marisol exhibited some of her first

sculptures in early 1950s group shows at the Tanager Gallery, and she was interested in King's work and in folk art. King did a delicate, folk-art-like portrait of her in 1955.

By the mid-1950s the sculptural climate had begun to change. Among older artists, Louise Bourgeois's totemlike wood figures, Joseph Cornell's luminous boxes, and Louise Nevelson's enigmatic collections of wood elements offered distilled, meditative alternatives to the gestural immediacy of welded metal sculpture. Richard Stanciewicz's welded "junk" sculptures, first seen in his one-artist debut in 1953, used direct-metal techniques but, "drawing more from a Dada than a Surrealist heritage . . . concentrated on a light-hearted and witty play on visual and verbal associations."[11] By the end of the decade, the interest in the anti-art aesthetic and anarchic humor of Dada had surfaced in the form of free-form events called Happenings. The new spirit was partly in reaction to the high seriousness of Abstract Expressionism, and partly in response to the presence in New York of avant-garde composer John Cage and grand-Dada Marcel Duchamp. By the mid-1950s Robert Rauschenberg, who had encountered Cage at Black Mountain College, was creating "combine paintings" and constructions such as Odalisk (1955–1958) [Fig. 1], which consisted of paint plus appropriated images and objects. His famous statement—"Painting relates to both art and life. Neither can be made. (I try to act in that gap between the two.)"—summarized the changing attitude of younger

artists, that art was where you found it and what you made it, rather than a given category. Rauschenberg had his first one-artist exhibition at the Betty Parsons Gallery in 1951, and his work was important to Marisol. She was also impressed by Jasper Johns's 1955 *Target with Four Faces* [Fig. 2]. Johns had begun attaching plaster casts of parts of his body to his paintings in 1955; his deliberately "cool" subjects prompted other artists to work from the outside in rather than from the inside out.

As a sequel to the 1951 "Ninth Street Show," the Stable Gallery inaugurated a series of "Annuals" in 1953; the fourth Stable Annual in 1955 included a Marisol sculpture that was similar to *Printer's Box* [Fig. 3]. She had begun making sculpture in 1953 after being intrigued by a 1951 exhibition of Pre-Columbian art in a New York gallery, and by a friend's collection of hand-carved and painted South American folk-art figures in boxes. She would later recall that turning from painting to sculpture "started as a kind of rebellion. Everything was so serious. . . . I started doing something funny so that I would become happier—and it worked."[12] Her work won the admiration of one reviewer of the Stable show: "Marisol's old type-box peopled with little clay figurines is a delight. There are lots of ideas in these niches and the very casualness is appealing."[13] Many of the tiny figures were single, but others were grouped in families, erotic couples, or mother-and-child pairs, subjects that would recur often in her subsequent work. The figures were placed in compartments like the elements in a Cornell box; the

Figure 2.
Target with Four Faces by Jasper Johns (born 1930), encaustic and collage on canvas with plaster casts, 1955. The Museum of Modern Art, New York; gift of Mr. and Mrs. Robert C. Scull

Figure 3.
Printer's Box by Marisol, white terra-cotta figures with bronze finial figures, not dated. Mrs. Edwin A. Bergman

Figure 4.
Untitled by Marisol, bronze, 1959.
Unlocated

appropriation of the wooden container was like Stanciewicz's recycling of junk, and the high unseriousness of the piece recalled Rauschenberg's rejection of individual expression.

By then Marisol had stopped painting, and within the next three years her sculpture appeared in three more Stable Annuals, a Stable exhibition of "New Sculpture," and a show of "New Work" at the Leo Castelli Gallery. In November 1957 she had her first one-artist exhibition at the Castelli Gallery. She exhibited "playful and erotic terra cottas, units fired individually and assembled like tiles . . . tiny clay figures pulling out from the surface like ducks caught in the mud. She thinks of them as having been influenced by Rodin's *Gates of Hell.* There were also free-standing terra cottas—active dabs of clay figures, wriggling upward in a kind of column. The rest of the show consisted of woodcarvings of animals and human figures."[14] A critic for the *New York Times* praised "her inventiveness and genuine originality."[15] Another had this to say: "Marisol, young Paris-born Venezuelan who has already impressed New York with tiny ritual-images in cubicles, appears in full repertory for her first one-man show; in her case, this means a search for identity that experimentally echoes both naif and primitive arts. Modernist lay-figures of Paris-New York lineage take 'family' form out of heavy, crudely carved and painted wooden planks, the best of which seem private totem poles. Her previous mannikins [sic] of terra cotta (Aztec out of Lipchitz) now collect in larger groups; lately

she has added abstract welding to what can be termed a creative pursuit of spiritual ancestors."[16]

An untitled work, which resembles a fountain [Fig. 4], is an example of her delicate welded-metal technique. At the same time she was constructing solid, planar pieces that combined weathered wooden boards, paint, and carving. *The Large Family Group* (1957) [Fig. 5], inspired by a coffee grinder in the shape of a man, is a cluster of five figures that has the appealing näiveté of folk art. Marisol had spent eight years in art school, but she had also been impressed by the expressiveness of untrained artists, and her early sculptural experiments were attempts to fuse her skills and interests effectively. Trying out various styles and experimenting with a widening range of materials, she was put off by the publicity that resulted from the Castelli exhibition. Her work was written up in a 1958 *Life* article called "Wood Carvers' Comeback" and, over the next two years, was included in group shows in New York, Pittsburgh, Chicago, and Spoleto, Italy. Meanwhile, she went to Rome, where she stayed until 1960. Later she said, "I got scared. . . . I thought, when you start getting publicity, you lose everything you have." She was also looking for "a better way of life—a more relaxed and happier one."[17]

"A microcosm of present-day society": 1960–1968

Returning to New York in 1960, Marisol showed some small bronzes at the Great Jones Gallery in 1961; one reviewer saw them as "con-

Figure 5.
The Large Family Group by
Marisol, wood, 1957. The Corcoran
Gallery of Art, Washington, D.C.; gift
of Mr. and Mrs. C. M. Lewis

glomerations of rambling,
scrambling little people."[18] Until
then her sculpture had consisted mainly of small-scale
modeled or painted figures, but
at that point she happened to
visit the Easthampton home of
painter Conrad Marca-Relli,
whose wife made hats. She
became intrigued by a potato
sack full of old wooden hat
forms that she found in the
garage. Taking them back to her
studio, she began to carve and
paint them and attach plaster
casts and found objects,
constructing larger-scale
ensembles. One of the first of
these sculptures was the
multiple *Self-Portrait* [Cat. no. 1],
which used seven of the hat
forms. Another of the new
works, *From France* [Fig. 6] was
described as: "Wood construction beam with painted and
stenciled wood, carved wood
hat forms, plaster castings, glass
eyes, baby shoe."[19] At the time,
Marisol was quoted as saying
that her sculpture represented
a man and a woman tourist
returning from France "with a
kiss and a handshake," and that
she had used plaster casts of
herself as parts of the figures
because she was available and "I
don't charge myself anything."[20]
She would offer this practical
explanation often in the early
1960s, but she later came to
see her use of self also as a
search for identity. *From France*
was included in the influential
1961 Museum of Modern Art
exhibition "The Art of Assemblage," and she was invited to
participate in a panel discussion
of assemblage at the Artists
Club. She took her place
among the four male panelists
wearing a white, Japanese-style
mask. When the audience
demanded that she remove it,
she did so, revealing her face

Figure 6. Left
From France by Marisol, mixed media, 1960. Unlocated

Figure 7. Right
Moon by Robert Indiana (born 1928), assemblage of wood and iron-rimmed wheels, 1960. The Museum of Modern Art, New York City; Philip Johnson Fund

made up to look exactly like the mask. The "mask behind the mask" became a Marisol legend. She was also famous for her reticence, and was reputed to have sat through a four-hour brunch without saying a single word.[21] She came to be known as the "Latin Garbo."[22]

The term "assemblage" was first used in 1953 by French painter Jean Dubuffet to distinguish his work from the early twentieth-century collages of Picasso and Braque. The assembling of everyday objects into three-dimensional arrangements or structures also had its origins in Marcel Duchamp's "Ready-mades" and Surrealist objects; by the late 1950s it had become an important activity for both European and American artists. Along with early twentieth-century pioneers, Dubuffet, Nevelson, Cornell, Rausch-enberg, and Johns were included in the show, as well as young British, French, German, Italian, Polish, Spanish, Swiss, and Yugoslavian artists. Americans John Chamberlain, Edward Kienholz, Lucas Samaras, H. C. Westermann, and Robert Indiana were also represented. Indiana's 1960 *Moon* [Fig. 7], made from a wood beam and iron and wood wheels, was particularly close to Marisol's work.

Like several other artists in the Assemblage exhibition, how-ever, Indiana came eventually to be more closely associated with Pop art, which also appropriates materials from the immediate environment, but without expressionistic intent. Devel-oped independently in England and New York in the late 1950s, it was called "Neo-Dada" and "OK Art" before the term "Pop," coined by British critic

Lawrence Alloway to describe
its popular-culture sources,
stuck to the art itself. The short
and snappy word proved
particularly descriptive of the
work of New York artists such
as Andy Warhol, Roy Lichten-
stein, Tom Wesselmann, James
Rosenquist, and Claes Oldenburg, who used "hard-edge
commercial techniques and
colors to convey their unmis-
takably popular, representa-
tional images."[23] This impersonal art seemed to have been
engendered by Johns, much as
expressive Assemblage had
been pioneered in New York
by Rauschenberg. Marisol had
been influenced by both, and
her relationship to Pop has
always been unclear. She had
many friends among the Pop
artists; she went to parties with
Andy Warhol and appeared in
two of his early movies. In
1962, the year Warhol created
his multiple portrait of Marilyn
Monroe, Marisol's media-
derived image of *John Wayne*
[Cat. no. 4] was featured in a
Life issue on the movies. She
also produced *Love,* a Pop
piece that incorporates an
actual Coca-Cola bottle. She
was not, however, included in
the important Sidney Janis
Gallery "New Realists" exhibition of 1962, where major
European and New York Pop
artists were presented together
for the first time. Nevertheless,
she has since been included in
essays on Pop sculpture (in, for
example, Wayne Andersen's
*American Sculpture in Process:
1930/1970*) and in books on
the movement, including Lucy
Lippard's 1966 *Pop Art* and *An
Illustrated Dictionary of Pop Art,*
which concluded that "Marisol
has contributed enormously to
the enrichment and scope of

Pop imagery."[24] Although her sculptures are based on mass-media images of popular figures and use mass-produced objects, her techniques have never been impersonal, and her work has elements of absurdity and irony that are unlike the deadpan literalness of hard-core New York Pop.

Marisol had a room of her own in the Museum of Modern Art's "Americans 1963," an exhibition that also included Indiana, Oldenburg, and Rosenquist. The Pop artists had "cutie-pie wit, an engaging decorativeness, and sometimes . . . a true billboard grandeur,"[25] whereas critic Katharine Kuh remarked on "the pathos, irony and outrageous satire with which [Marisol] invests her sculpture. Whether she designs a single figure or a large group, she invariably ends up with a biting comment on human foibles. . . . No one has deflated human pomposity with greater insight."[26] Her interest in social satire had also been noted in reviews of her first solo exhibition of the larger-scale pieces at the Stable Gallery in the spring of 1962. The show included *The Bathers* [Fig. 8], a sculpture that was one of the first to create its own self-contained environment. There were also three portraits that incorporated actual barrels: her artist friend *Ruth* [Cat. no. 2]; *John*, a man on a rocking horse (the hat reminded her of Pope John XXIII's headgear); and a double, mounted portrait of George Washington and Simon Bolívar as *The Generals* [Fig. 9]. The rigid frontality and hieratic poses of *The Kennedys* [Fig. 10] reminded one reviewer of royal Egyptian portraits, and although the exhibition as a whole was

Figure 9.
The Generals by Marisol, wood and mixed media, 1961–1962. Albright-Knox Art Gallery, Buffalo, New York; gift of Seymour H. Knox, 1962

"very sophisticated, strong and accurate," such pieces were "bizarre and perhaps a little cruel . . . more like effigies than figures."[27] The stiffness and satire of the Kennedy portrait contrasted strongly with the tenderness of *The Family* [Fig. 11], which was also in the Stable show. Based on a photograph "of a poor American family from the South, of the type shown in Walker Evans's portraits of Alabama tenant farmers during the Depression," the mother-dominated group is reminiscent of the 1957 *Large Family Group,* but enlarged to life-size and given three-dimensional details.[28] Marisol has returned to the subject of the one or two-parent family throughout her subsequent work.

In 1964 she had a second Stable Gallery exhibition that proved to be immensely popular with the public: it was seen by two thousand people a day, and more on Saturdays. The portrait of John Wayne was on view, along with those of Andy Warhol [Cat. no. 3], *The Generals,* and a portrait of a portrait: her version of Leonardo da Vinci's *Mona Lisa,* painted on a found board to which she added folded plaster hands. For her, as for Marcel Duchamp, Andy Warhol, and other modern artists, the mystery of Leonardo's art could best be dealt with by remaking his most famous works. There were several multiple self-portraits—*The Bathers, The Wedding, Dinner Date*—and groups of four to six figures (most with her features) riding in a car, playing in a jazz band, sitting on a sofa (*The Visit*), walking a dog, or wheeling two wooden babies in a real

Figure 10. Above
The Kennedys by Marisol, mixed media, 1960. Israel Museum, Jerusalem

Figure 11. Right
The Family by Marisol, mixed media, 1962. The Museum of Modern Art, New York City; Advisory Committee Fund

Figure 12.
The Family by Marisol, mixed
media assemblage, 1963. Milwaukee
Art Museum, Minnesota; on loan
from the Robert B. Mayer Family
Collection

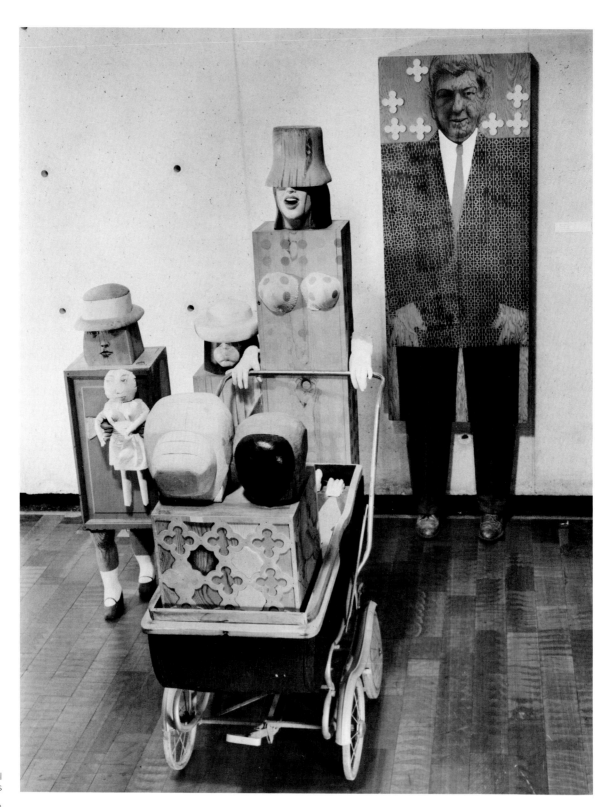

Figure 13.
Baby Girl by Marisol, wood and mixed media, 1963. Albright-Knox Art Gallery, Buffalo, New York; gift of Seymour H. Knox, 1964

carriage. This *Family* [Fig. 12] is on a middle-class outing, and the bratty offspring, stylish but mindless mother, and peripheral father are wryly satirized. The doll held by the eldest child is a small, stuffed Marisol, like those clutched by the six-foot high *Baby Girl* [Fig. 13] and the seven-foot *Baby Boy*. The monstrous babies reminded one viewer of Goya's *Saturn*,[29] but Marisol recently noted that "The boy represented America, holding me—young America, still a little irresponsible."[30] Although most of the works included self-portraits, the multiple images of the artist were most provocative in *The Wedding*, where Marisol married Marisol—"I finally made it legal," she said—and in *Dinner Date* [Fig. 14], where she dined with herself off cafeteria trays in a spoof on her supposedly glamorous life-style.[31] The proliferation of Marisols could be seen negatively as "this turning inward, this self-absorption,"[32] or positively by those who saw her using herself as "a microcosm of present-day society."[33] She was also criticized for lack of attention to content—"she mixes allusions, parody, and quotations, cutting across iconography indiscriminately,"[34]—and to three-dimensional form: "There is no form to begin with, only mute mummifications."[35]

As if to confound or compound all criticism, in 1965 and 1966 Marisol created a group of sculptures whose subjects were almost exclusively women with her features. (She also used elements of her face for the males in *Couple #1, Couple #2, The Dealers,* and *The Party*.) While this might have seemed a further step in the direction of

narcissism, the new works were actually more abstract, emphasizing bold shapes, flat surfaces, and simpler content.

In January 1965, an *Arts* magazine article by Richard Wollheim on "Minimal Art" had given a name to an emerging movement that aimed at reducing sculpture and painting to basic abstract shapes and eliminating narrative or figurative subject matter. Sculptors such as Donald Judd, Robert Morris, and Tony Smith were creating boxlike, repetitious structures, emphasizing the "single most important sculptural value—shape."[36] Marisol did not become a Minimal sculptor, but she admired the idea: "I wish I had thought of that . . . if I removed the heads and ornaments from my work, I would have minimal sculpture."[37] The new works, shown at the Sidney Janis Gallery in 1966, were more form-conscious and cerebral than the assemblages of the earlier 1960s. Even the titles were generic: *Woman with Flower Pot, Six Women, Women Leaning*. The most elaborate piece was *The Party* [Fig. 15], a wall-to-wall environment filled with thirteen guests and two servants (all Marisols) that has become one of her best-known works. The women wear ballgowns and elaborate hairdos; the beehive shape of one suggests the elongated head of Nefertiti, while another wears a "crown" made from an earlier sculpture. One face consists of a smiling photograph of Marisol, and one is dominated by the Cyclopean eye of a tiny television set. A reviewer described the group as "frozen in an elegant trance as if they were creatures in a dollhouse awaiting the touch of

Figure 14.
Dinner Date by Marisol, mixed
media, 1964. Yale University Art
Gallery, New Haven, Connecticut; gift
of Susan Morse Hilles

Figure 15.
The Party by Marisol, mixed media,
1965–1966. Minneapolis Institute of
Arts, Minnesota; on loan from the
collection of Mrs. Robert B. Mayer

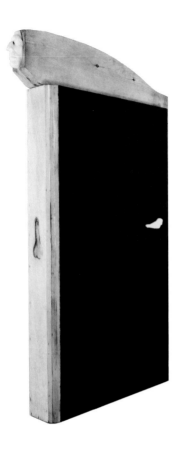

a magic wand to bring them to life."[38] Others saw self-absorption or a critique of the emptiness of high society, but the artist recently said of the piece: "In the 60's there was a rebellion against what was proper and boring. . . . I wanted to satirize the new society, but I really liked the people. I did a lot of self-portraits then because it was a time of searching for one's identity. I looked at my faces, all different in wood, and asked, *Who am I?*"[39]

In 1967 she turned again to images of others. Her earlier portraits had often been affectionate portrayals of art-world friends, but she did only two such pieces in 1967–1968: a sleek, cigarette-lighter shaped portrait of her boyfriend *Guy* [Fig. 16], and a tongue-in-cheek image of her dealer, *Sidney Janis Selling Portrait of Sidney Janis by Marisol, by Marisol* [Cat. no. 12]. The double likeness of Janis was reminiscent of her only 1965 portrait, that of curator Henry Geldzahler [Cat. no. 5].

That year she also ventured into the complicated field of public sculpture for the first time. Hers was one of seven maquettes considered for a bronze statue of Father Joseph Damien de Veuster, the nineteenth-century Belgian priest who died of leprosy at forty-nine, after working for sixteen years in the leper colony on the Hawaiian island of Molokai trying to eradicate the disease. The statue was to be one of two that would represent Hawaii in the National Statuary Hall in the United States Capitol. Controversy arose when the judges failed to reach a unanimous decision in her favor and public opinion was solicited by putting

Figure 17.
Father Damien by Marisol, bronze, 1967. United States Capitol, Washington, D.C.

Figure 18.
The Rt. Hon. Harold Wilson by Marisol, mixed media, 1967. Private collection

the maquettes on exhibition. Found "shocking" because it represented an older Father Damien [Fig. 17] whose face was already marked by the disease that would kill him, her design was rejected by the Hawaiian House of Representatives in favor of a more idealized figure, but through the efforts of the Hawaiian Senate, it was reinstated two months later.[40] The statue was installed in 1968.

Meanwhile, *Time* commissioned several portraits for the cover of the magazine, including *Hugh Hefner* [Cat. no. 7] and *Bob Hope* [Cat. no. 8]. At the same time, the London *Daily Telegraph Magazine* suggested that she do a series of eminent Britishers. She went to England to explore the possibilities, and decided on the *Royal Family* [Cat. no. 11] and a portrait of the Right Honorable Harold Wilson, who was then Prime Minister. She saw her subjects in person, although from afar, but created the portraits, as usual, from photographs. *Harold Wilson* [Fig. 18] is as minimal as the 1965–1966 sculptures: a smooth, rounded head and a single, waving hand sit atop a simple box whose shape was likened to that "of an unusually healthy pouter pigeon—or an Egyptian mummy."[41] She also internationalized the original idea by going on to make sculptures of French President Charles de Gaulle [Cat. no. 6], China's Chairman Mao Tsetung, American President Lyndon B. Johnson [Cat. no. 9], and Spain's Generalissimo Francisco Franco. *Franco* [Fig. 19] "seemed so unreal, I was going to make him all out of paper that folded," she said, and paper was used for the hat,

Figure 19.
Generalissimo Francisco Franco by Marisol, mixed media, 1967. Private collection

hands, white gloves, insignia, and epaulets.[42] The head consists of "a scrap of paper, some pencil and black crayon. . . . She closed the paper loop with a monster's stitch of staples, then wet and pinched it for eye bags, neatly stapled some creases into jowls."[43] Her "Figures of State" were exhibited at the Hanover Gallery in London, where there was some indignation, especially over the *Royal Family*. In New York, on the other hand, a reviewer of the show at the Sidney Janis Gallery commented that "perhaps the theme was too rigidly tailored to suit her penetrating satire . . . both de Gaulle and LBJ have the disadvantage, from the artist's standpoint, of already being ready-made art objects."[44]

LBJ, who was represented with his wife and daughters, and the *Royal Family* had been her first family groups since the satiric *Family* of 1963. She went on to make the autobiographical *Mi Mama y Yo* (1968) [Cat. no. 13] from an old family photograph. Although it became one of her favorite pieces, she did not return to the theme of the family again until 1978. Included in more than a dozen exhibitions between 1966 and 1968, her work was beginning to achieve international stature. In 1968 she was one of five women included in the Los Angeles County Museum of Art's seventy-six-artist exhibition "American Sculpture of the Sixties." In the same year she was, ironically, prevented by her lack of American citizenship at that time from representing the United States at the XXXIV Venice Biennale. She represented Venezuela instead, exhibiting eight major sculptures done between 1961 and 1968;

they were also shown at the Museum Boymans-van Beuningen in Rotterdam that year. She had already had an exhibition of work done between 1956 and 1965 at the Arts Club in Chicago in 1965, and in 1970 and 1971 there would be two more retrospectives, at Philadelphia's Moore College of Art and at the Worcester Art Museum.

In 1958 she had left the success of her first solo exhibition to spend eighteen months in Rome; in 1968 she left the United States again for more than a year, traveling to South America, the Caribbean coast, India, Nepal, Thailand, and Cambodia. She also visited Tahiti, where she learned scuba diving and underwater photography. She later would say: "People in the West think their art is better. . . . I went to Asia, and I couldn't believe the art they have there. . . . I had never seen anything like that, not even in Europe. I was influenced there. I went to Angkor Wat, and it was really a surprise. It shocked me."[45]

The exposure to Asian art and culture came at a critical moment in her life. Between 1960 and 1968 she had become a well-known sculptor whose unique combinations of painting, carving, and assemblage were included in major international exhibitions and bought by important museums and collectors. She had created portraits of some of the best-known people of the decade, along with satiric images of herself and others in the restricting roles prescribed by Western society. Now she would pursue the answer to the question of identity in other ways.

Figure 20.
Trigger Fish I by Marisol, mixed
media, 1970. Collection of the artist

"Something very pure": 1970–1977

Returning to New York in 1970, Marisol found that the art scene had changed. Although most of the Pop artists were still working in their familiar styles, many Minimalist sculptors had begun to create massive landscape projects, soon to be known as Earthworks, in remote corners of the world. Others were moving toward Conceptual art, in which ideas rather than objects were the main products. As an offshoot of this movement, some "Performance" artists were beginning to use their own bodies as art forms. Marisol had already done this, in her own satirical way, in mid-1960s pieces such as *The Party*. Now, as she said, "I felt like doing something very pure, just for the sake of it. . . . I wanted to do something very beautiful."[46] The result was a school of large stained and varnished mahogany fish, most bearing a mask of her face, that somewhat baffled those accustomed to her wry social criticism when they were shown at the Sidney Janis Gallery in 1973. One reviewer said curtly, "Apart from autobiographical implications, there were no explanations . . . for the sudden appearance of these new slippery fish."[47] Some of them, such as the *Barracuda* [Cat. no. 16] were dangerous predators, while others, such as *Green Fish* [Cat. no. 15] and *Trigger Fish I* [Fig. 20], were elegant, streamlined shapes that echoed her 1960s concern for form, but in a more organic way.

Also indicative of her interest in nature, rather than culture, were the untitled pastel landscape drawings that were shown with the fish. She had always done drawings in preparation for, along with, and as part of her sculptures, but in the early 1970s she focused intensely on graphics, making prints and "a series of disturbingly explicit and autobiographical erotic drawings."[48] A retrospective exhibition of her prints from 1961 through 1973 at the New York Cultural Center included the life-size, double-page lithograph *Diptych*. Derived from a body print of the artist, it represented a female nude endowed with long flowing hair and fantastic touches such as extra hands and feet and a toothy wound on the left side. In 1972, while she was in the midst of making these private images, *Time* asked her to do a double portrait of Richard Nixon and Henry Kissinger [Cat. no. 17] for the cover of the magazine; it was the only portrait she produced between 1968 and 1977. Her work continued in an erotic, imaginative, and highly personal vein through the mid-1970s. In 1975 she exhibited new graphics and a group of wall pieces at the Sidney Janis Gallery. The wall pieces were made of plaster masks of her face with Coke bottles, beer cans, light bulbs, and keys dangling from them. In *I Have Been Here 24 Years* fetishlike objects attached to pieces of rope hang around and in front of the face like ritual offerings. The years between 1970 and 1977 were ones of intense autobiographical explorations in which "Marisol focuses on the interconnectedness of humans with nature and the contemporary with the archaic."[49]

"A sense of timelessness": 1977–1989

After 1975 Marisol stopped using casts of her face as part of her sculpture. She began a series of roughly carved portraits of older artists whom she admired, beginning with painters Pablo Picasso and Georgia O'Keeffe, and choreographer Martha Graham. The stocky, muscular *Picasso* [Fig. 21] is a powerful figure made magical by its two sets of hands; one viewer noted that "a knot of twisted nails, embedded in the uncarved block of his chest . . . reveals the found nature of Marisol's materials and refers to Picasso's own ingenious use of discarded objects in his sculptures."[50] By 1981 she had done a second O'Keeffe (with antelopes), as well as artists Willem de Kooning [Cat. no. 19], Marcel Duchamp, and Louise Nevelson, writer William Burroughs, and composer Virgil Thomson. All the figures are seated: Duchamp in a high-backed chair, O'Keeffe on a rock, Thomson at a carved grand piano. Marisol felt that the older people would have a favorite place to sit, but the pose also works symbolically, for these people are enthroned actually as well as in our mind's eye. Seeing them in the Sidney Janis Gallery in 1981, one reviewer said, was like "walking through a Hall of Kings."[51] She also included a 1977 seated portrait of her father [Fig. 22], a benign, relaxed presence that was very unlike the magnetic, dreamlike *Mi Mama y Yo* of 1968. The new portraits of women were descended from the portrait of her mother, and were among her most powerful. *Georgia O'Keeffe with Dogs* [Cat. no. 18] depicts an ancient

Figure 21. Above left
Picasso by Marisol, wood and mixed media, 1977. Private collection

Figure 22. Above right
Portrait of My Father by Marisol, wood and plaster, 1977. Collection of the artist

Figure 23.
Portrait of Martha Graham by
Marisol, bronze, wood, and plaster,
1977. Private collection

queen guarded by symmetrical beasts. Martha Graham [Fig. 23] is majestically upright despite hands twisted with rheumatism (Marisol knotted her own hands with string before casting them and attaching them to the piece). Enduring strength is echoed in the portrait of Louise Nevelson [Fig. 24]. She is shown wearing her familiar cape, firmly planted on a low platform before black panels that "suggest the Nevelson black wall sculptures that established her artistic reputation."[52] The new portraits, which she called "Artists and Artistes," were well received. One critic wrote that, "Like Egyptian sculpture, they seem to contain the spirit of the individual, conferring a sense of timelessness to the transitory."[53] Another concluded that the works "successfully join a public iconography with an extremely personal statement."[54]

These serious, personal homages grew out of her introspective explorations of the 1970s; the single, isolated figures, expressively carved from rough chunks of plain wood, were very unlike the boxy, colorful groups done in the 1960s. She also began to re-image certain themes in her new expressionistic style. For example, she had not created a large family group since the 1967 *Royal Family,* but along with the artist portraits her version of Leonardo's *Virgin, Child, St. Anne and St. John* (1978) [Fig. 25] emerged as a roughly carved invocation of that most mysterious of "families." In 1983 she portrayed *Stephanie's Family* [Fig. 26] as a large group with a calm, Madonna-like woman at its center. More recently, she

Figure 24.
Portrait of Louise Nevelson by
Marisol, pencil and oil on wood and
plaster, 1981. Private collection

constructed a large-scale ensemble called *Poor Family I* (1986) [Fig. 27]; in this dignified yet pathetic portrait of three generations of an impoverished, anonymous family, the imaginary dustbowl imagery of her 1962 *Family* becomes a wider sympathy for the real problems of the Third World.

A large "family" was also the subject of her recent version of Leonardo da Vinci's *The Last Supper* [Fig. 28], a thirty-foot-long sculpture in wood, stone, plywood, and plaster. She had already made her own versions of two other famous Leonardo paintings; the *Last Supper* is her most monumental homage to another artist. When the sculpture was shown at the Sidney Janis Gallery in 1984, one critic experienced "pure, uncomplicated pleasure at her feat of gentle audacity."[55] At the center is the isolated, immovable figure of Jesus, carved from salvaged brownstone. Around Him the disciples react to the news that one of them will betray Him, and to the dramatic institution of the Eucharist. Assembled from laminated plywood, chunks of carved wood, and plaster casts, each disciple is a unique commingling of two- and three-dimensional forms that is faithful to the individualized emotions in the original painting. Judas, the fourth from the left, has a head "carved from a solid beam of nearly black wood so dense that Marisol's blade would barely cut it. The metaphor is a remarkably nice one: Evil is denser and tougher—more obdurate—than good."[56] Indeed, for her, "the piece symbolized the downfall of Western culture, the loss of morality. I inserted myself

Figure 25.
Virgin, Child, St. Anne and St. John by Marisol, charcoal on wood, plaster, and stone, 1978. Museo de Arte Contemporaneo, Caracas, Venezuela

Figure 26.
Stephanie's Family by Marisol,
wood, charcoal, and plaster, 1983.
Private collection

Figure 27.
Poor Family I by Marisol, wood,
charcoal, stone, and plastic doll, 1986.
Private collection

Figure 28.
The Last Supper by Marisol, painted and drawn wood, plywood, brownstone, plaster, and aluminum, 1984 (detail from **Self-Portrait Looking at the Last Supper**). The Metropolitan Museum of Art, New York City; gift of Mr. and Mrs. Roberto C. Polo, 1986

Figure 29.
Mark Twain by Marisol, bronze, 1983. Collection Wave Hill, Riverdale, Bronx, New York

because I am watching it happen."[57] A seated portrait of the artist broods in front of her creation. However, one critic thought that "taking the Leonardo as a subject is a Warholish thing to do, and the irony—or is it impishness—is compounded by the addition of a spectator."[58]

She has not, however, swung back to self-portraiture, but has continued her explorations of others through an ongoing series of ambitious portraits that now includes nineteenth-century figures. The 1984 exhibition included not only a contemporary portrait (of a businessman standing next to his large wooden airplane), but also portraits of Abraham Lincoln and writer Mark Twain. The small bronze *Mark Twain* [Fig. 29], standing between a huge bird and cats, is a magical and mysteriously potent figure. The symbolic conjunction of people and animals is also evident in her recent *John, Washington, and Emily Roebling Crossing the Brooklyn Bridge for the First Time* [Fig. 30]: Emily holds up a huge rooster as a symbol of victory and authority. "It was she," said Marisol, "who actually finished the [Brooklyn] bridge."[59] A large-scale wood version of this impressive, imaginative group portrait was done pending the completion of the bronze commemorative monument sponsored by the Brooklyn Heights Association.

The Roebling family and a stately portrait of *Emperor Hirohito with Empress Nagako* [Cat. no. 21], inspired by a trip to Japan, were on view in her most recent exhibition at the Sidney Janis Gallery. In *Sari Dienes* [Fig. 31], however, she returned to the affectionate

Figure 30.
John, Washington, and Emily Roebling Crossing the Brooklyn Bridge for the First Time by Marisol, wood, plaster, and stain, 1989. Sidney Janis Gallery, New York City

portrayal of art-world friends that had begun with *Ruth* and *Andy* in the early 1960s. A combination of "Artists and Artistes" homage and personal fantasy, the portrait envisioned the artist, now in her nineties, as a child with masses of curly hair, mounted on a rocking horse-unicorn. It reflects the continuities as well as the changes in Marisol's art, as does her powerful sculpture of South African *Bishop Desmond Tutu* [Cat. no. 20]. His stem, righteous portrait was placed in a room with *Poor Family I* and *Poor Family II* (1987). Her acute social and political consciousness had inspired the *Kennedys* and the "Figures of State" in the 1960s; now she addresses herself to larger issues of world hunger and oppression. Her current projects include sculptures having to do with these problems, as well as several portraits and public commissions.

High in an aerie overlooking the Hudson River, Marisol goes on quietly making sculpture. Her spartan lower Manhattan loft is lined with windows at one end and with carpenter's tools at the other. Like a bird looking for nest-building materials, she forages in forgotten corners of the city, finding an old wooden pier or the chunk of battered brownstone that became the figure of Jesus in her *Last Supper.* Immersing herself in materials, she meditates long and hard on the construction of her complex pieces. As she said, in speaking of a recent work that took two years to complete: "I live with my art a long time."[60]

She has become a mature artist with a uniquely expressive and imaginative approach to

Figure 31.
Portrait of Sari Dienes by Marisol,
wood, plaster, and charcoal, 1987.
Private collection

portraiture and to sculpture itself. Her work combines painting, drawing, carving, casting, assemblage, and other techniques in lively, unpredictable, and subversive ways. Her portraits always present not only a person, but also a point of view. A figurative bent and a wry, topical humor have made her sculpture accessible, but underneath is an artist who can beguile us into taking a serious second look at ourselves and our society.

Notes

1. Paul Gardner, "Who Is Marisol?" *Art News* 88 (May 1989): 147.

2. *Ibid.*

3. Quoted in Lawrence Campbell, "The Creative Eye of the Artist: Marisol," *Cosmopolitan* 156 (June 1964): 68.

4. Jeff Goldberg, "Pop Artist Marisol—20 Years After Her First Fame—Recalls Her Life and Loves," *People* 3 (March 24, 1975): 40.

5. Quoted in Grace Glueck, "It's Not Pop, It's Not Op—It's Marisol," *New York Times Magazine*, March 7, 1965, p. 40.

6. *Ibid.*

7. Hans Hofmann, *Search for the Real* (Cambridge, Mass., 1967), p. 50.

8. "Marisol," *Time* 81 (June 7, 1963): 76–77.

9. The "Irascibles" included painters Willem de Kooning, Adolph Gottlieb, Ad Reinhardt, Hedda Sterne, Richard Pousettte-Dart, William Baziotes, Jackson Pollock, Clyfford Still, Robert Motherwell, Bradley Walker Tomlin, Theodoros Stamos, Jimmy Ernst, Barnett Newman, James Brooks, and Mark Rothko.

10. Wayne Andersen, *American Sculpture in Process: 1930/1970* (Boston, 1975), p. 108.

11. *Ibid.*, pp. 101–2.

12. Quoted in Glueck, "It's Not Pop," p. 45.

13. John Ferren, "Stable State of Mind," *Art News* 54 (May 1955): 24.

14. Lawrence Campbell, "Marisol's Magic Mixtures," *Art News* 63 (March 1964): 38.

15. Quoted in Charles Moritz, ed., *Current Biography* (New York, 1968), p. 242.

16. "Reviews and Previews: Marisol," *Art News* 56 (November 1957): 14.

17. Quoted in Glueck, "It's Not Pop," p. 48.

18. Vivien Raynor, "In the Galleries: Marisol," *Arts* 35 (May–June 1961): 94.

19. William Seitz, *The Art of Assemblage* (New York, 1961), p. 161.

20. Millicent Browner, "Sculptress, Own Model, Is 'A Beatnik' No Longer," *Indianapolis Star*, November 22, 1961.

21. Edward Barry, "The Art of Marisol: Intriguing Objects Fashioned of Wood," *Chicago Tribune*, December 22, 1965, p. 9.

22. Glueck, "It's Not Pop," p. 48.

23. Lucy Lippard, *Pop Art* (New York, 1966), p. 69.

24. José Pierre, *An Illustrated Dictionary of Pop Art* (London, 1975), p. 99.

25. Thomas B. Hess, "The Phony Crisis in American Art," *Art News* 62 (Summer 1963): 26.

26. In Museum of Modern Art, *Americans 1963* (New York, 1963), p. 68.

27. Vivien Raynor, "In the Galleries: Marisol," *Arts* 36 (September 1962): 44.

28. Roberta Bernstein and Yoshiaki Toro, *Marisol* (Tokyo, 1989), unpaged.

29. Brian O'Doherty, "Marisol: The Enigma of the Self-Image," *New York Times*, March 1, 1964, p. 23.

30. Quoted in Gardner, "Who Is Marisol?" p. 149.

31. Quoted in John Gruen, "Art: Marisol—Top to Bottom," *New York Herald Tribune*, March 8, 1964.

32. *Ibid.*

33. Katharine Kuh, "The Fine Arts: Notes of a Peripatetic Gallerygoer," *Saturday Review* 47 (April 25, 1964): 71.

34. Max Kozloff, "New York Letter: Marisol," *Art International* 6 (September 1962): 35.

35. Sidney Tillim, "In the Galleries: Marisol," *Arts* 38 (April 1964): 28.

36. Robert Morris, "Notes on Sculpture," in Gregory Battcock, ed., *Minimal Art* (New York, 1968), p. 228.

37. Quoted in Jacqueline Barnitz, "The Marisol Mask," *Artes Hispanicas* 1 (Autumn 1967): 47.

38. "Art: Sculpture—The Dollmaker," *Time* 85 (May 28, 1965): 80.

39. Quoted in Gardner, "Who Is Marisol?" pp. 149–50.

40. "How to Portray a Martyr?" *Time* 89 (May 12, 1967): 83.

41. Ian Ball, "Figures of State," *Daily Telegraph Magazine* (London), September 15, 1967, p. 20.

42. Quoted in Daniel Chapman, "Marisol—A Brilliant Sculptress Shapes the Heads of State," *Look* 23 (November 14, 1967): 82.

43. *Ibid.*

44. "Reviews and Previews: Marisol," *Art News* 66 (November 1967): 60.

45. Quoted in Cindy Nemser, *Art Talk* (New York, 1975), p. 186.

46. *Ibid.*, p. 190.

47. April Kingsley, "New York Letter," *Art International* 17 (October 1973): 53.

48. Roberta Bernstein, "Marisol's Self-Portraits: The Dream and the Dreamer," *Arts* 59 (March 1985): 89.

49. *Ibid.*

50. Deborah C. Phillips, "New York Reviews: Marisol," *Art News* 80 (September 1981): 231.

51. Stephen Westfall, "Arts Reviews: Marisol," *Arts* 55 (June 1981): 26.

52. Bernstein and Toro, *Marisol.*

53. Roberta Bernstein, "Marisol as a Portraitist: Artists and Artistes," *Arts* 55 (May 1981): 115.

54. Joan Simon, "Chers maîtres," *Art in America* 69 (October 1981): 121.

55. Kay Larson, "Supper with Marisol," *New York Magazine* 17 (June 4, 1984): 70.

56. *Ibid.*

57. Quoted in Gardner, "Who Is Marisol?" p. 150.

58. Vivien Raynor, "Art: Marisol Sculpture from Leonardo Painting," *New York Times,* June 1, 1984, p. C20.

59. Grace Glueck, "Marisol Shows Her Brooklyn Bridge Memorial," *New York Times,* April 16, 1988, p. 11.

60. Quoted in Gardner, "Who Is Marisol?" p. 146.

Catalogue of the Exhibition

1. **Self-Portrait**

Mixed media, 1961–1962
110.5 cm. (43½ in.)
Museum of Contemporary Art;
promised gift of Joseph and Jory
Shapiro

Marisol created her first self-portrait in 1957, using a cast of her face made by an artist friend.[1] Between 1961 and 1975 she used parts of herself in most of her sculptures, but the purpose was more often social criticism than autobiography. This tongue-in-cheek self-portrait is no exception. It was also one of her first large-scale pieces, inspired by the discovery of some old wooden hat forms that she used as heads.

Here the seven carved and painted heads have been provided with hats, hairstyles, and expressions that range from the grotesque to the elegant. She said, "I looked at my faces, all different in wood, and asked, *Who am I?* "[2] To look from one to another of these faces is to see seven radically different people, but they share a collective rectangular body. Part of its wood has been left bare—a modest left hand covers some of the bareness—and part has been painted primary red, yellow, and blue, the favorite Pop colors. Like her 1963 *Baby Girl,* she sits directly on the floor, with six bare legs sticking stiffly out before her. One critic commented that the effect was like "a row of people in the stocks of Newgate Prison."[3] The restraints of social role-playing are invisible but very real; this imaginative image presents them and circumvents them at the same time.

2. **Ruth** (Kligman) born 1931
Mixed media, 1962
167.6 cm. (66 in.)
Rose Art Museum, Brandeis
University; Gevirtz-Mnuchin
Purchase Fund

Artist Ruth Kligman met painter
Jackson Pollock at the Cedar Bar in
New York early in 1956.[4] On
Saturday, August 11, she went to
visit him at his summer home in
eastern Long Island, taking her
friend Edith Metzger with her. That
night Pollock lost control of the car
in which he and the two women
were traveling, and it crashed,
killing both him and Metzger. Ruth
Kligman was injured, but she
survived.

Marisol's portrait of her friend
incorporates an actual barrel, as
did the 1961–1962 *John* and *The
Generals*. One critic noted that "it
reminded one of the type of rural
American humor in which people
have their clothes stolen while in
swimming and go home dressed in
barrels."[5] The curving barrel also
suggests Kligman's voluptuous
figure. Supported by four pairs of
legs, the torso has multiple breasts
and cast-plaster hands attached to
it like the extremities of a Hindu
deity. Repetition of a body, or
parts thereof, goes back to Rodin's
Three Shades (1881), but few
contemporary sculptors other than
Marisol have tapped its expressive
potential. Other portraits in the
exhibition—*Self-Portrait, Henry,* and
Sidney Janis—use the same device.

3. **Andy** (Warhol) 1928–1987
Mixed media, 1962–1963
143.5 cm. (56½ in.)
Mrs. Edwin A. Bergman

Andy Warhol was a media
celebrity, one of a handful of artists
whose face became, if anything,
even better known than his work.
At the time of this portrait,
however, he had just made his
entrance as a Pop painter, after
working for many years as a
commercial artist. Both he and
Marisol had solo exhibitions at the
Stable Gallery in 1962, and both
were very much part of the New
York art scene. They went to
openings and parties together, and
Marisol appeared in two of
Warhol's early films.

The portrait captures a basic
quality of Warhol's personality:
"Andy remains essentially a
voyeur, letting things take their
course and looking on with cool
detachment, interested but
uninvolved."[6] Or, as one of his
entourage put it: "Talking to him is
like talking to a chair."[7] He sits
impassively, in a pose that Marisol
would use again for a 1977–1981
series of homages to older artists
such as Willem de Kooning [Cat.
no. 19]. In this case, however,
Warhol's face and body are simply
repeated in paint on all the surfaces of a cube, whose planes are
interrupted only by a pair of folded
plaster hands and the toes of a
pair of shoes. When viewed from
the front of the sculpture, the
shoes provide the figure with an
extra left foot. The bland unknow-
ability of the image recalls
Warhol's statement: "If you want
to know Andy Warhol, just look at
the surface of my paintings and
films and me, and there I am.
There's nothing behind it."[8]

4. **John Wayne** 1907–1979
Mixed media, 1963
264.2 cm. (104 in.)
Colorado Springs Fine Arts
Center; Julianne Kemper Gilliam
Purchase Fund, Debutante Ball
Purchase Fund

In 1962 and 1963 John Wayne
appeared in six films, including John
Ford's *The Man Who Shot Liberty
Valence.* Wayne had been a star
since he played the Ringo Kid in
Ford's 1939 *Stagecoach,* and they
had made many movies together.
By the time of this portrait Wayne
was a national icon; his screen
portrayals of tough, genial,
independent Westerners had
made him the embodiment of the
all-American hero. In keeping with
this persona, Marisol has shown
him larger than life but almost as
two-dimensional as his screen
image: the horse was cut from
plywood sheets, with stacked
boxes on top and added cutouts
for arms, legs, gun, and hat.

The portrait was commissioned by
Life for a special issue on the
movies, and the magazine noted
that he "makes a patriotic
appearance in blue jeans and white
saddle on a blazing red horse."[9]
Under a ten-gallon yellow hat, his
deadpan movie face appears on
two sides of his cubic head, but a
smiling publicity photograph is
pasted on the front, and on the
back he has been drawn "as he
appears in tuxedo at premieres."[10]
Yet his draw is so fast that an extra
right hand raises a gun while it is
still held at his side. Wayne was a
mass-culture symbol of Americana,
and his portrait looks like a cross
between a merry-go-round figure
and a weathervane. It has the
cheerful innocence and instant
appeal of folk art, infused with
Marisol's sophisticated wit.

5. **Henry** (Geldzahler) born 1925
Mixed media, 1965
170.2 cm. (67 in.)
Mr. and Mrs. Brooks Barron

Henry Geldzahler joined the
curatorial staff of the Metropolitan
Museum of Art in 1960, when he
was twenty-five; he became
curator of the newly formed
Department of Twentieth-Century
Art in 1967. In the early 1960s he
showed great interest in and
enthusiasm for the work of young
New York artists and got to know
emerging talents such as Marisol,
Andy Warhol, Claes Oldenburg,
and Frank Stella. At the Metropolitan he was curator of large-scale
contemporary exhibitions such as
"New York Painting and Sculpture:
1940–1970." He would later serve
as New York City's commissioner
of the Department of Cultural
Affairs.

Most of Marisol's sculpture in 1965
and 1966 concerned groups of
female figures presented in a
minimal style that emphasized
basic shapes and flat surfaces; this
was the only portrait she produced during those two years.
Consisting of a rectangular box
topped by two bulbous heads, it
depicts Geldzahler as both actor
and spectator. On the left he is
shown stepping forward, and his
features are blurred as though he
were turning his head very quickly.
On the right he stands, a passive
onlooker, with arms folded and
eyes hidden by real sunglasses.
Marisol was interested in the
different roles a person plays
simultaneously; in 1966 fifteen
versions of herself attended *The
Party*, and in 1968 she portrayed
Sidney Janis [Cat. no. 12] as both
an art dealer and an art object.

6. **Charles de Gaulle** 1890–
1970
Mixed media, 1967
272.4 cm. (107¼ in.)
National Museum of American
Art, Smithsonian Institution; gift of
Mr. and Mrs. David K. Anderson,
Martha Jackson Collection

As the spokesman for Free France
during World War II and as
president of the Fifth French
Republic from 1958 to 1969,
General Charles de Gaulle played
a vital role in international politics
for thirty years. His stern face and
tall, commanding figure became
familiar to the world. Marisol has
made him even taller by placing
him on a delicate black-and-gold
carriage. The device recalls the
wheeled bases of Giacometti's
figures, as well as the triumphal
chariots of nineteenth-century
commemorative monuments.

Indeed, the artist's "first thought
was to stand him in a chariot.
Then she came upon an early
picture of him in a graceful open
carriage that seemed too frail to
carry its majestic burden."[11] As the
portrait proceeded, everything
about de Gaulle became outsize.
"When she carved him a pair of
ears that were roughly in propor-
tion, they looked wrong. They had
to be flaring and king-sized."[12] The
general's nose and jowls, even the
huge pockets of his baggy khaki
uniform, are scaled to the mon-
umentality of the figure.

As in many Marisol portraits, there
is also a touch of the absurd. From
de Gaulle's left shoulder waves a
small white plaster hand that
counteracts the high seriousness of
the image and complicates the
emotions of the viewer. As one
critic commented, "Reaction to le
Grand Charles in wood is
mixed—a sudden laugh that ends
in silence. He is both monumental
and ludicrous."[13]

7. **Hugh Hefner** born 1926
Mixed media, 1967
185.4 cm. (73 in.)
National Portrait Gallery,
Smithsonian Institution; gift of Time
Inc.

In 1967 Hugh Hefner was named
Magazine Man of the Year by the
Magazine Industry Newsletter, and
Time published a long article on
the founder of *Playboy* and the
Playboy business empire. Marisol
was asked to create a portrait of
Hefner for the cover. *Time* had
been enthusiastic about her
sculpture ever since it had
appeared in the Museum of
Modern Art's "Americans 1963"
exhibition. She was described as
an artist "whose creations are
specifically designed to appeal to
that part of the mind in which
fantasy and reality seem identi-
cal."[14]

The portrait of Hefner, like most
of Marisol's work from the mid-
1960s, consists of the minimum
number of simple, basic shapes.
His casually dressed body is
painted on the front and back of a
hollow wooden box. Seen from
the front, he is standing with
folded arms, but from the back he
appears to be stepping forward.
An elongated, streamlined head
balances on top; features are
represented only on its front
surface.

When the portrait was delivered
to the magazine, the editors had
questions for the artist: "Why the
red, white, and blue? 'Perhaps he's
the All-American Boy.' The
tucked-under hand—on the right
when the work is viewed from the
front—pokes out on the wrong
side in back. Was it a mistake? 'No,
I like to make things absurd.' And
the two pipes? 'He has too much
of everything.' "[15]

8. **Bob Hope** born 1903
Wood, 1967
48.3 cm. (19 in.)
National Portrait Gallery,
Smithsonian Institution; gift of Time
Inc.

Marisol's first *Time* portrait—*Hugh
Hefner* [Cat. no. 7]—was used on
the cover of the magazine in
March 1967. By December, when
the colorful *Bob Hope* appeared
on the cover of the Christmas
issue, she had done many other
portraits, notably the world leaders
of her "Figures of State" series.
Bob Hope is a departure from
these and earlier portraits, in which
a whole person is invoked through
pose, gesture, media-derived
images, and significant objects.

In this case, she chose to portray
only the head and shoulders of the
famous comedian, focusing on his
mobile, expressive features and
distinctive nose. Hope is shown in
action: alert and smiling, he turns
his head and opens his mouth to
deliver one of his incomparable
one-liners. The stop-motion effect
is unlike Marisol's usual distilled,
iconlike images, but it perfectly
captures Hope's stage entrance:
"The crooked grin spreads wide,
the clear brown eyes stay cool,
and the audience roars its
welcome."[16] The drawing is
realistic, almost caricature-like, but
the portrait holds its own as a
sculptural object through the
faceting that enlivens its wooden
surfaces.

9. **LBJ** 1908–1973
Mixed media, 1967
203.2 cm. (80 in.)
The Museum of Modern Art; gift of Mr. and Mrs. Lester Avnet, 1968

Vice President Lyndon B. Johnson was sworn in as President when President John F. Kennedy was assassinated on November 22, 1963, and he was returned to that office by the election of 1964. Johnson implemented measures to achieve the "Great Society," including the Civil Rights Act of 1964 and the Voting Rights Act of 1965, but did not run for a second term in 1968.

In 1967 London's *Daily Telegraph Magazine* suggested that Marisol make portraits of prominent people. She produced *The Royal Family* [Cat. no. 11] and Prime Minister Harold Wilson and went on to sculpt other "Figures of State," including *Charles de Gaulle* [Cat. no. 6] and *LBJ*. Unlike the others, Johnson seems to stride forward, but the figure remains imprisoned in a wooden box reminiscent of Egyptian mummy cases. Although he is as static and severe as a pharaoh, Johnson wears a businessman's plain blue suit and carries no clues to his high office. The image was based on Marisol's perception that "The atmosphere is more business-like since the change of Presidents. The world is not a happy place anymore."17

But Johnson holds three birds in the palm of his left hand; "Marisol modeled them on grey house wrens, nature's busybodies."18 Bearing the features of Lady Bird, Lynda Bird, and Luci Baines Johnson, the three tiny, smiling faces also add a note of cheerful fantasy to the basic sobriety of the portrait.

10. **Nelson Rockefeller** 1908–1979
Grey slate, 1967
37.4 cm. (14¾ in.)
National Portrait Gallery,
Smithsonian Institution; gift of Time
Inc.

Nelson A. Rockefeller was four times governor of New York State and was Vice President of the United States from 1974 to 1977. Characterized as "capable, ambitious, idealistic—and also arrogant," he had aspirations to the presidency that were never realized.[19] A member of one of America's wealthiest families, he was also a major collector of paintings, sculpture, and primitive art. The portrait was one of several commissioned by *Time* in 1967 [see also Cat. nos. 7 and 8], but it did not appear on the cover of the magazine until September 1974, when President Gerald Ford presented Rockefeller as his nominee for Vice President.

This was Marisol's first stone portrait, and she has said that the material was brittle and difficult to carve. She chose the material as a pun on the governor's nickname: "Rocky." The stone has been flatly treated in areas such as the hair, but realistic lines and wrinkles are carved around the features, and Rockefeller is shown with his characteristically jovial public expression. His features are portrayed only on the front surface of the block, so the face has a masklike two-dimensionality. However, it is surrounded by an outline, cut as deeply as Egyptian sunk relief, that casts a three-dimensional shadow without liberating the face from the surface. The style is in keeping with much of Marisol's sculpture in the mid-1960s, which emphasized simple shapes and flat surfaces.

11. **The Royal Family**
Mixed media, 1967
304.8 cm. (120 in.)
Miami University Art Museum; gift
of Paul and Mona Doepper

The family has been one of
Marisol's most recurrent subjects.
In 1957 she painted *The Large
Family Group* on boards, and in
1962 she grouped five imaginary
dustbowl figures in *The Family*. She
returned to the theme with a
sculpture of a middle-class family in
1964; although *The Royal Family*
was done as part of her 1967
"Figures of State" series, it also
represents an aristocratic version
of her basic family group.

She had seen the family from a
distance, but portrayed them from
photographs showing them in
casual clothes: "the sort of clothes
they wear at Sandringham—every
artist seems to show them on
State occasions in tiaras and
uniforms."[20] Queen Elizabeth II,
however, wears a terra-cotta
crown made from a Marisol
sculpture of the 1950s. She has
also been provided with an extra
right hand that waves from her
shoulder like Charles de Gaulle's.
Prince Philip remains in the
background, but the smiling Prince
of Wales and Princess Anne are
painted on one large block, and
small Princes Andrew and Edward
are at the front with the royal
Corgi. "A royal red carpet literally
reaches up into their lives,
guaranteeing deep-pile ameni-
ties."[21] When *The Royal Family*
was exhibited in London at the
Hanover Gallery in 1967, "an
impassioned segment of Britain's
middle class protested the artist's
version of the House of Windsor
as a bland, middle-class gaggle of
'squares and blockheads.' "[22]

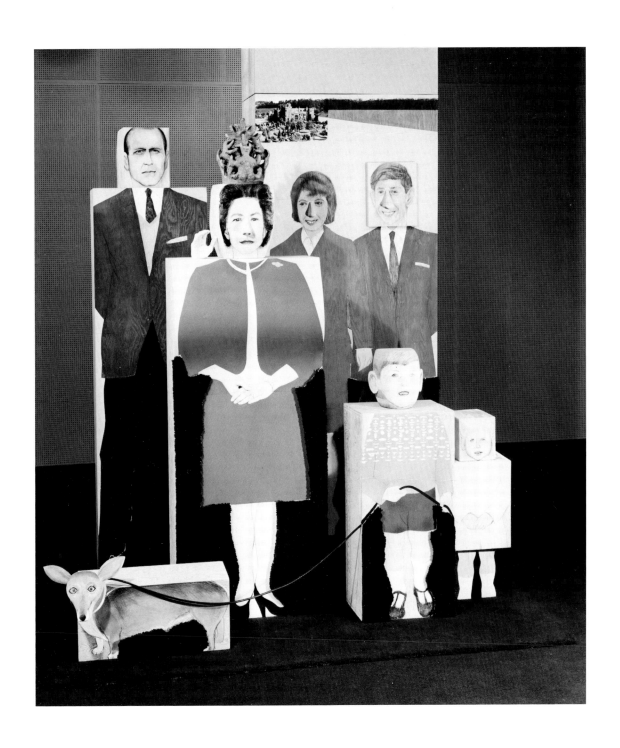

12. **Sidney Janis Selling Portrait of Sidney Janis by Marisol, by Marisol**
Mixed media, 1967–1968
175.3 cm. (69 in.)
The Museum of Modern Art; the Sidney and Harriet Janis Collection, 1967

Sidney Janis (1896 –1989) was a major collector of modern art who became an organizer of exhibitions and an author; among his books were the important *Abstract and Surrealist Art in America* (1944) and *Picasso: The Recent Years, 1939–1946*. In 1948, at the age of fifty-two, he founded the Sidney Janis Gallery, where he "mounted significant shows of European masters and helped put Abstract Expressionism on the international map . . . in the 1960s he played an important role in the growth of Pop art."[23]

Marisol joined his gallery in 1966, after having solo exhibitions at the Castelli and Stable galleries, and having been included in many important group shows. She portrayed her dealer as the consummate salesman, with his head thrust aggressively forward but with a relaxed plaster hand holding (real) glasses on his knee as he prepares to discuss the fine points of the blocky figure of himself standing next to him. This second Janis consists of a faceted polygonal bust, reminiscent of her portrait of Bob Hope [Cat. no. 8], resting on a box that has the rest of the figure painted on the front. The double image recalls her 1965 sculpture of Henry Geldzahler [Cat. no. 5], but here the active-passive duality of that portrait is raised to an imaginative and affectionate level.

13. **Mi Mama y Yo**
Steel and aluminum, 1968
185.4 cm. (73 in.)
Collection of the artist

Marisol has created many images of a woman (or women) with one or more children. In the 1960s most of these figures were given her face but were not real self-portraits; even *Self-Portrait* [Cat. no. 1] was more of a spoof on social roles than anything else. In 1967, however, she spent considerable energy on several portraits for the cover of *Time* and on a series of portraits called "Figures of State." The following year she undertook *Mi Mama y Yo,* her first truly autobiographical sculpture. She portrayed herself as a stern child in a pink dress, standing on a bench and holding a parasol over her smiling, seated mother. Her mother, Josefina Hernandez Escobar, died when Marisol was eleven; the portrait was done from an old family photograph. It combines Marisol's mid-1960s abstraction—the two bodies could be pieces of minimal sculpture—with realistic details, such as the mother's elaborate hair and openwork red shoes, which suggest vividly painful memories. The portrait "poignantly and with ambivalent feelings harks back to the artist's childhood."[24] It initiated a time of intense self-inquiry that would last until 1977, when Marisol made a portrait of her father and then embarked on a series of homages to older artists. She has refused to part with *Mi Mama y Yo* for, as she says, "the imagery and meaning are too personal for me."[25]

14. **White Dreams**
Mixed media, 1968
24.1 cm. (9½ in.)
Hood Museum of Art, Dartmouth College; bequest of Jay R. Wolf, class of 1951

Marisol once said: "A work of art is like a dream where all the characters, no matter in what disguise, are part of the dreamer."[26] In art and in dreams, one can be anything. Earlier in the 1960s, she had portrayed herself as a humorously multiple personality, and as people from many different aspects and levels of society. Now she began to imagine herself more directly, in the childhood-inspired *Mi Mama y Yo* [Cat. no. 13] and in this self-portrait. She has, however, also said that the darkened mask of her face in *White Dreams* was an allusion to the hopes of black people; the white carnation could be read as an ironic reference to Spanish dancers with flowers in their teeth. In art and in dreams, one can be anything and everything all at once.

Unlike most of Marisol's work, *White Dreams* is a relief made to be hung on the wall, rather than a free-standing sculpture. An earlier relief-like portrait—*Nelson Rockefeller* [Cat. no. 10]—was actually part of a solid chunk of stone. This self-portrait was among her first wall pieces; she went on to create a series of them in the mid-1970s, using plaster casts of her face combined in unusual and expressive ways with ordinary objects.

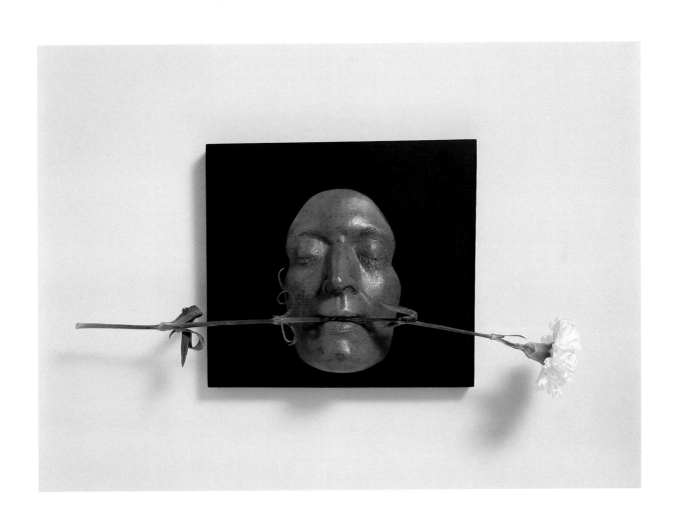

15. Green Fish (above)
Wood, varnish, plastic, and plaster,
1970
47 cm. (18½ in.)
Collection of the artist

This sculpture is one of a series of
fish/self-portraits that Marisol
created between 1970 and 1973.
In 1968, after completing *Mi
Mama y Yo,* Marisol had left New
York. She traveled to South and
Central America and to India and
Southeast Asia, and was much
impressed by the people and the
art she encountered there. For a
time, she stayed on the island of
Tahiti, where she learned to scuba
dive. When she returned to New
York in 1970, she began work on
nine large-scale mahogany fish,
which were exhibited at the
Sidney Janis Gallery in 1973. The
wood is stained green, brown, or
black and given many coats of
varnish to achieve a mirrorlike
surface. The forms are as elegantly
clean-cut as in her mid-1960s
sculptures and, as in many earlier
figurative pieces, most of the fish
have plaster Marisol faces. Here,
however, the effect is not
humorous but haunting.

One critic noted that "Combining
human and animal images is an
ancient practice, so it pops up
again and again in art and
dreams."[27] *Green Fish* is particularly
dreamlike, for its sleek shape and
open-mouthed face fit together in
an illogical but convincing way;
even the delicate fin-hands seem
natural to this beautiful, inexpli-
cable hybrid.

16. Barracuda (below)
Wood, varnish, and plastic, 1971
58.4 cm. (23 in.)
Collection of the artist

The fish/self-portraits of the early
1970s startled fans of Marisol's
1960s tongue-in-cheek social
commentary. Serious, personal,
and dreamlike, they were radically
different from her earlier portraits.
One critic saw them as "post-Pop"
and declared that these compos-
ites "would have been a good
choice for inclusion in a Surrealist
exhibition."[28] Indeed, *L' invention
collective,* a 1935 painting by
Belgian Surrealist René Magritte,
depicts a beached creature whose
lower body is that of a human
female and whose upper half is
that of a fish—a nightmarish
reversal of the fairy-tale mermaid.

Marisol's equally unexpected
hybrids were expressions of a wish
to create "something beautiful and
dangerous."[29] And, as she noted
elsewhere, "The shark and the
barracuda are the most beautiful.
They scare you, and so they must
have impressed me."[30] She also
carved three very long, very thin
Needlefish, but the *Barracuda*'s
streamlined shape is the most
effective. By giving this predator
her face, she humanized its power
and, at the same time, endowed
herself with its swift strength. The
magical and potent fusion of
human and animal has not
reappeared in her subsequent
work; the fish emerged from a
period of autobiographical
exploration.

17. **Henry Kissinger and Richard Nixon**

Pink marble, 1972
35.6 cm. (14 in.)
National Portrait Gallery,
Smithsonian Institution; gift of Time
Inc.

In 1972 *Time* asked Marisol to
create a portrait of President
Richard Nixon (born 1913) and
Assistant for National Security
Affairs Henry Kissinger (born
1923), whom the magazine was
going to name "Men of the Year"
for their efforts to achieve "a new
global design, a multipolar world in
which an equilibrium of power
would ensure what Nixon called 'a
full generation of peace.' "[31] Their
activities that year included Nixon's
presidential visit to Moscow and
Kissinger's announcement that a
Vietnam "peace is at hand."

Marisol had recently returned from
a trip around the world, which had
included a stay in Southeast Asia,
where she found the art and the
people very beautiful. She was now
carving large-scale fish [Cat. nos. 15
and 16] and doing many autobiographical drawings and prints. She
said she had lost interest in the
public: "I don't want to reach them.
. . . They look ugly to me. . . .
Suddenly I made a portrait of
Nixon, and it was like a nightmare
thinking about this person. I would
go into the subway, and everybody
had that face—the very tight lips
and sort of grayish complexion. I
really would have nightmares at
night."[32] *Nelson Rockefeller* had
been her first portrait in stone;
here she used a chunk of marble
for the two heavy-jowled faces
locked together like stubborn
Siamese twins. The rough carving
of the marble anticipates the
expressive approach to materials
that she would develop in the later
1970s.

18. **Georgia O'Keeffe with Dogs**

Wood, 1977
133.4 cm. (52½ in.)
Collection of the artist

From 1929 on, American painter Georgia O'Keeffe (1887–1986) spent several months of each year in New Mexico. Even before she settled in Abiquiu in 1949, her transcendent art was associated with the openness and austere beauty of the Southwestern landscape. Although her work began to be fully appreciated only when she was in her seventies, her status as a major twentieth-century artist has grown ever since. She was ninety when Marisol created this portrait of her, after meeting and spending several days with her in New Mexico.

The sculpture was one of the earliest in a 1977–1981 series of homages to revered older "Artists and Artistes": painters Pablo Picasso, Marcel Duchamp, and Willem de Kooning, sculptor Louise Nevelson, choreographer Martha Graham, writer William Burroughs, and composer Virgil Thomson. Each was seated in a characteristic pose and context: "There sat Georgia O'Keeffe on a tree stump, flanked by her two chows, looking off into the distance (it's hard to imagine O'Keeffe at home indoors)."[33] Marisol now carved the elements roughly and expressively from plain chunks of old wood. One critic noted that "Concentrated around O'Keeffe's tightly drawn mouth, fine, straight nose and intent eyes is a wrinkled pattern of carved furrows that gives way to the polished surfaces of her head. Such textural variations bring greater accuracy and subtlety to Marisol's interpretations."[34]

19. **Willem de Kooning**

born 1904
Charcoal and oil on wood and
plaster, 1980
152.4 cm. (60 in.)
Joseph D. and Janet M. Shein

Marisol met painter Willem de
Kooning in New York in the 1950s.
He had had his first solo gallery
exhibition in 1948, and by the early
1950s was known as one of the
most powerful of the Abstract
Expressionists. Marisol was influenced by certain older artists as well
as by her contemporaries: "de
Kooning was my hero—actually, he
is still my hero—and I learned a lot
from him."[35] He apparently was
also fond of her: "Willem de
Kooning once broke up a furious
artistic debate by throwing his arms
around Marisol and shouting, 'I love
you; you're so quiet.'"[36]

The portrait was one of her 1977–
1981 "Artists and Artistes" homages. The series, exhibited at the
Sidney Janis Gallery in 1983, also
included *Georgia O'Keeffe* [Cat. no.
18]. De Kooning is shown seated in
his favorite chair, an elaborately
carved but comfortable rocker that
enfolds and enthrones him like a
king. His smiling face is roughly
carved from old wood, the features
enlivened with touches of charcoal
and oil paint. His hands, cast from
his own, rest on the chair arms, with
an extra one on his knee (*Picasso*, in
the same series, was given two
extra hands).[37] When the sculpture
was exhibited, one critic compared
it with the 1967 portrait of Sidney
Janis, concluding that the earlier
piece was "an image more than an
actual presence," while the "carved
features in the de Kooning convey a
more vivid and profound sense of
the individual."[38]

20. **Bishop Desmond Tutu**

born 1931
Wood, stain, and fluorescent light,
1988
190.5 cm. (75 in.)
Sidney Janis Gallery

Bishop Desmond Tutu's ongoing campaign against apartheid in South Africa made Marisol decide to make a portrait of him, because "I'm interested in him. I like what he's doing. And I think I've always been interested in politics."[39] Her political and social consciousness was evident in early 1960s pieces such as *The Kennedys* and *The Family*, and developed further through the 1967 "Figures of State" and portraits for *Time*. Recently, Marisol has become concerned about world hunger and oppression and has created groups such as *Mother and Child with Empty Bowl* (1984). At the Sidney Janis Gallery in 1989, the Tutu portrait was placed in a room with the 1986–1987 *Poor Family I* and *Poor Family II*.

The "body is formed by a massive rectangular box painted purple to resemble a cassock, and on his chest he wears a cutout cross lighted from within the box. His realistic head, beautifully carved from a pier beam, is cocked atop the abstract body, and against it rests his carved hand, unattached to an arm, holding the elaborate sceptre of his office."[40] The heavy staff, wall-like body, massive head, and glowing cross all add to the aura of power that emanates from this larger-than-life-size portrait.

21. **Emperor Hirohito with Empress Nagako**

Wood, clay, paint, and fluorescent light, 1989
193 cm. (76 in.)
Sidney Janis Gallery

The sixty-two-year reign of Emperor Hirohito (1901–1989), now known as the Showa era, was one of the most eventful in the long history of Japan. During that time, "his nation embraced militarism, conquered much of Asia, waged war on the Allied Powers, suffered the world's first atomic bombing, and painfully rebuilt, rising in just four decades to become the world's most vibrant economic power."[41] He symbolized the perpetuation of the country's ancient traditions in the tumultuous twentieth century. This memorial portrait of the Emperor with Empress Nagako (born 1903) was done in 1989, the year Marisol had her first solo exhibition in Japan.

Her 1967 *Royal Family* had been depicted in casual clothes, grouped together on a red-carpeted platform. In *Emperor Hirohito with Empress Nagako,* however, the royal couple are portrayed in formal ceremonial dress, raised high on a two-step dais. They are dignified and distant, with blocky bodies that resemble elegant chess pieces. Only the Empress's delicate plaster hands, the Emperor's glowing eyes, and the pair's expressively carved wooden heads counteract the impression of inaccessible, enigmatic icons.

Notes

Self-Portrait
1. Roberta Bernstein, "Marisol's Self-Portraits: The Dream and the Dreamer," *Arts* 59 (March 1985): 89.

2. Quoted in Paul Gardner, "Who Is Marisol?" *Art News* 88 (May 1989): 150.

3. Lawrence Campbell, "Marisol's Magic Mixtures," *Art News* 63 (March 1964): 38.

Ruth
4. B. H. Friedman, *Jackson Pollock* (New York, 1972), p. 232.

5. Campbell, "Marisol's Magic Mixtures," p. 38.

Andy
6. John Coplans, *Andy Warhol* (New York, 1970), p. 14.

7. Victor Bockris, *Andy Warhol* (New York, 1989), p. 207.

8. Museum of Modern Art, *Andy Warhol Retrospective* (New York, 1989), p. 457.

John Wayne
9. "John Wayne, Who Rides Off Artfully in All Directions," *Life* 55 (December 20, 1963): 111.

10. *Ibid.*

Charles de Gaulle
11. Ian Ball, "Figures of State," *Daily Telegraph Magazine* (London), September 15, 1967, p. 20.

12. *Ibid.*

13. Daniel Chapman, "Marisol . . . A Brilliant Sculptress Shapes the Heads of State," *Look* 23 (November 14, 1967): 79.

Hugh Hefner
14. "Marisol," *Time* 81 (June 7, 1963): 77.

15. "A Letter from the Publisher," *Time* 89 (March 3, 1967): 4.

Bob Hope
16. "The Comedian as Hero," *Time* 90 (December 22, 1967): 58.

LBJ
17. Chapman, "Marisol," p. 78.

18. *Ibid.*

Nelson Rockefeller
19. "A Natural Force on a National Stage," *Time* (September 2, 1974): 18.

The Royal Family
20. Ball, "Figures of State," p. 20.

21. Chapman, "Marisol," p. 81.

22. *Ibid.*, p. 80.

Sidney Janis Selling Portrait of Sidney Janis by Marisol by Marisol
23. Grace Glueck, "Sidney Janis, Trend-Setting Art Dealer, Dies at 93," *New York Times*, November 24, 1989, p. 8.

Mi Mama y Yo
24. Bernstein, "Marisol's Self-Portraits," p. 87.

25. Quoted in Gardner, "Who Is Marisol?" p. 149.

White Dreams
26. Quoted in Campbell, "Marisol's Magic Mixtures," p. 40.

Green Fish
27. John Perrault, "The Identity Behind Marisol's Face," *Village Voice*, May 17, 1973, p. 47.

Barracuda
28. Kingsley, "New York Letter," p. 53.

29. Quoted in Gardner, "Who Is Marisol?" p. 147.

30. Quoted in Nemser, *Art Talk*, p. 191.

Henry Kissinger and Richard Nixon
31. "Nixon and Kissinger: Triumph and Trial," *Time* 101 (January 1, 1973): 13.

32. Quoted in Nemser, *Art Talk*, pp. 190–91.

Georgia O'Keeffe with Dogs
33. Joan Simon, "Chers maîtres," *Art in America* 69 (October 1981): 121.

34. Deborah C. Phillips, "New York Reviews: Marisol," *Art News* 80 (September 1981): 231.

Willem de Kooning
35. Avis Berman, "A Bold and Incisive Way of Portraying Movers and Shakers," *Smithsonian* 14 (February 1984): 57.

36. Barbara Gold, "Portrait of Marisol," *Interplay* 1 (January 1968): 52.

37. Roberta Bernstein, "Marisol as Portraitist: Artists and Artistes," *Arts* 55 (May 1981): 114.

38. *Ibid.*

Bishop Desmond Tutu
39. Grace Glueck, "Marisol Shows Her Brooklyn Bridge Memorial," *New York Times*, June 1, 1984, p. C20.

40. *Ibid.*

Emperor Hirohito with Empress Nagako
41. Susan Chira, "Hirohito, 124th Emperor of Japan, Is Dead at 87," *New York Times*, January 7, 1989, p. 1.

Appendix

Exhibitions of Marisol's Work

Solo Exhibitions

1957	Leo Castelli Gallery, New York
1962	Stable Gallery, New York
1964	Stable Gallery, New York
1965	Arts Club of Chicago
1966	Sidney Janis Gallery, New York
1967	Sidney Janis Gallery, New York
	Hanover Gallery, London
1968	"XXXIV Venice Biennale," Italy—represents Venezuela
	Guild Hall, Easthampton, New York
1970	Moore College of Art, Philadelphia
1971	Worcester Art Museum, Massachusetts
1973	The New York Cultural Center
	Sidney Janis Gallery, New York
1974	Trisolini Gallery, Ohio University, Athens; Columbus Gallery of Fine Arts, Ohio
1975	Sidney Janis Gallery, New York
	Makler Gallery, Philadelphia
1977	Contemporary Arts Museum, Houston
1981	Sidney Janis Gallery, New York
1984	Sidney Janis Gallery, New York
1988	Boca Raton Museum of Art, Florida
	Dolly Fiterman Gallery, Minneapolis
1989	Sidney Janis Gallery, New York
	Galerie Tokoro, Tokyo

Selected Group Exhibitions

1958	Festival of Two Worlds, Spoleto, Italy
1959	"The 1959 Pittsburgh International," Museum of Art, Carnegie Institute
	"Pan American Art," The Art Institute of Chicago
	"Work in 3 Dimensions," Leo Castelli Gallery, New York
1961	"The Art of Assemblage," Museum of Modern Art, New York; Museum of Contemporary Art, Dallas; Museum of Art, San Francisco
	"Marisol and Howard Kanowitz," Great Jones Gallery, New York
1962	"Recent Acquisitions," Museum of Modern Art, New York
	"Annual Exhibition of Sculpture and Drawings," Whitney Museum of American Art, New York
1963	"66th American Annual," The Art Institute of Chicago
	"Americans 1963," Museum of Modern Art, New York
	"Mixed Media and Pop Art," Albright-Knox Art Gallery, Buffalo, New York
	"The Art of Things," Jerrold Morris Gallery, Toronto
1964	"Painting and Sculpture of a Decade," Tate Gallery, London; Institute of Contemporary Art, Philadelphia
	"New Realism," Municipal Museum, The Hague
	"Boxes," Dwan Gallery, Los Angeles
	"Annual Exhibition," Whitney Museum of American Art, New York
	"3 Generations," Sidney Janis Gallery, New York
	"The 1964 Pittsburgh International," Museum of Art, Carnegie Institute; Washington Gallery of Modern Art, Washington, D.C.

"Between the Fairs," Whitney Museum of American Art, New York

1965   "The New American Realism," Worcester Art Museum, Massachusetts

"Op and Pop," Sidney Janis Gallery, New York

1966   "The Harry N. Abrams Family Collection," The Jewish Museum, New York

"Erotic Art '66," Sidney Janis Gallery, New York

"Latin American Art Since Independence," traveling exhibition sponsored by Museum of Modern Art, New York

"New Art in Philadelphia," Institute of Contemporary Art, Philadelphia

"68th American Exhibition," The Art Institute of Chicago

"Art of the United States: 1670–1966," Whitney Museum of American Art, New York

"Whitney Annual: Sculpture and Prints," Whitney Museum of American Art, New York

"Tribute to Frank O'Hara," Museum of Modern Art, New York

1967   "American Sculpture of the Sixties," Los Angeles County Museum of Art; Philadelphia Museum of Art

"The 1967 Pittsburgh International," Museum of Art, Carnegie Institute

"Sculptures in Environment," New York Outdoors Show

"Homage to Marilyn Monroe," Sidney Janis Gallery, New York

1968   "The Sidney and Harriet Janis Collection," Museum of Modern Art, New York

"Word and Image," Museum of Modern Art, New York

"American Drawings 1968," Moore College of Art, Philadelphia

"The Obsessive Image," Institute of Contemporary Art, London

"Art of Ancient and Modern Latin America," Isaac Delgado Museum of Art, New Orleans

"Documenta IV," Kassel, Germany

1969   "7 Artists," Sidney Janis Gallery, New York

"Arts 69—Helsinki," Art Gallery of Ateneum, Finland

"Pop Art Redefined," Hayward Gallery, London

"Contemporary American Drawing," Fort Worth Center Museum, Texas

"Modern International Sculptures," Hakone Open Air Museum, Japan (first prize)

"29th Annual Exhibition," The Art Institute of Chicago

1970   "Carnegie International Exhibition of Painting and Sculpture," Museum of Art, Carnegie Institute, Pittsburgh

"L'Art Vivant Américain," Fondation Maeght, Paris

"Contemporary Women Artists," Nathern Gallery, Skidmore College, Saratoga Springs, New York; National Arts Club, New York

"7 Artists," Sidney Janis Gallery, New York

1971   "Abstract Expressionism and Pop Art," Sidney Janis Gallery, New York

"Modern International Sculpture," Hakone Open Air Museum, Japan

"Art Around the Automobile," Emily Lowe Gallery, Hofstra University, New York; Institute of Contemporary Art, Philadelphia; Rice University, Houston

1972   "Colossal Scale," Sidney Janis Gallery, New York

"Contemporary Women Artists," State University at Potsdam, New York

1973   "Drawing Exhibition," Baltimore Museum of Art

"Selected Editions," Sidney Janis Gallery, New York

Basel Art Fair 4, Sidney Janis Gallery, Switzerland

"Jewelry as Sculpture as Jewelry," Institute of Contemporary
    Art, Boston

1974   "Twenty-fifth Anniversary, Part II," Sidney Janis Gallery, New
        York

"Sculpture in the Park," North Jersey Cultural Council

1975   "6 Americans," Sidney Janis Gallery, New York

"The Art Students League of New York 100th Anniver-
        sary," Kennedy Galleries, New York

"Realism and Nudity," Künsthalle, Darmstadt, Germany

"The Nude in America," The New York Cultural Center;
        Minneapolis Institute of Art; University of Houston Fine
        Arts Center

"Vistas Contemporaneas Latino-Americanas," New Jersey
        State Council on the Arts, Trenton

1976   "The Golden Door: Artist-Immigrants of America, 1876–
        1976," Hirshhorn Museum and Sculpture Garden, Washing-
        ton, D.C.

"Dada/Surrealist Heritage," Sterling and Francine Clark Art
        Institute, Williamstown, Massachusetts

"The Year of the Woman: Reprise," The Bronx Museum of
        Arts

1977   "Women Artists 1976: A Celebration," McNay Art Institute,
        San Antonio, Texas

"Contemporary Women: Consciousness and Content," The
        Brooklyn Museum Art School

1978   "7 Americans," Sidney Janis Gallery, New York

"Award Recipient Exhibition," American Academy and Institute of Arts
        and Letters, New York

"Another Aspect of Pop Art," P.S.1, Long Island City, New
        York

1979   "The Opposite Sex: A Realistic Viewpoint," University of
        Missouri, Columbia

"de Kooning, Marisol, Pearlstein, Grossman, Hanson," Miami–
        Dade Community College, Florida

1980   "Four from Janis," Hope Makler Gallery, Philadelphia

1981   "Sculptors' Drawings," Max Hutchinson Gallery, New York

"Bronze," Hamilton Gallery, New York

"Romantic Drawings," Alex Rosenberg Gallery, New York

"New Dimensions in Drawing," Aldrich Museum of Contem-
        porary Art, Ridgefield, Connecticut

1983   "American Women Artists Part I: 20th Century Pioneers,"
        Sidney Janis Gallery, New York

1984   "New Portraits," Institute for Art and Urban Resources, P.S.1,
        Long Island City, New York

"Soul Catchers," Stellweg Seguy Gallery, New York

"Drawings Since 1974," Hirshhorn Museum and Sculpture
        Garden, Washington, D.C. .

"Masters of the Sixties," Marisa del Re Gallery, New York

"Ways of Wood," Sculpture Center, New York

1985   "Feminists and Misogynists Together at Last," Avenue B
        Gallery, New York

"Wood, Water, and Stone," 909 Third Avenue, New York

"Forms in Wood: American Sculpture of the 1950s,"
        Philadelphia Art Museum

"Dorothy C. Miller, with an Eye to American Art," Smith
        College Museum of Art, Northampton, Massachusetts

"In Three Dimensions: Recent Sculpture by Women," Pratt
        Institute, New York

"Sights for Small Eyes," Heckscher Museum, Huntington, New
        York

"American Women Artists," Peck School, New York

"The Gathering of the Avant-Garde: The Lower East Side,
        1950–1970," Kenkeleba House, New York

"Body and Soul: Recent Figurative Sculpture," Contemporary Arts Center, Cincinnati

1986   "Drawings by Sculptors," Nohra Haime Gallery, New York

"Pop: Then and Now," Castle Gallery, New Rochelle, New York

1987   "Monte Carlo Sculpture '87," Marisa del Re Gallery, New York

"The Artist's Mother: Portraits and Homages," Heckscher Museum, Huntington, New York; National Portrait Gallery, Washington, D.C.

1988   "Just Like a Woman," Greenville County Museum of Art, Greenville, S.C.

"The New Sculpture Group: A Look Back 1957–1962," New York Studio School, New York

"XLIV Venice Biennale," Italy

"Urban Figures," Whitney Museum of American Art at Philip Morris, New York

"Centennial Exhibition of the National Association of Women Artists," Nassau County Museum, New York

1989   "100 Drawings by Women," Hillwood Art Gallery, Long Island University, Brookville, New York; USIA—Pan America and Europe

"Body Fragments," Shea and Beker Gallery, New York

"Positive I.D.," Southern Alleghenies Museum of Art, Loretto, Pennsylvania

1990   "Body Language! The Figure in the Art of Our Time," Rose Art Museum, Brandeis University, Waltham, Massachusetts

Selected Bibliography

Books and Catalogues

Andersen, Wayne. *American Sculpture in Process: 1930/1970*. Boston: New York Graphic Society, 1975.

Arts Club of Chicago. *Marisol*. Chicago: Arts Club, 1965.

Ashton, Dore. *Modern American Sculpture*. New York: Abrams, 1968.

————. *American Art Since 1945*. New York: Oxford University Press, 1982.

Berkson, Bill, ed. *In Memory of My Feelings—A Selection of Poems by Frank O'Hara*. New York: Museum of Modern Art, 1967.

Bernstein, Roberta, and Yoshiaki Toro. *Marisol*. Tokyo: Galerie Tokoro, 1989.

Burnham, Jack. *Beyond Modern Sculpture*. New York: George Braziller, 1968.

Calas, Nicolas and Elena. *Icons and Images of the Sixties*. New York: E. P. Dutton, 1971.

Craven, Wayne. *Sculpture in America*. New York: Thomas Y. Crowell, 1968.

Creeley, Robert. *Presences: A Text for Marisol*. New York: Scribner's, 1976.

Diament de Sujo, Clara. "The Itinerary of Marisol." In *XXXIV Biennale*. Venice: XXXIV Biennale, 1968.

Estudio Actual. *Marisol*. Caracas: Estudio Actual, 1973.

Gablik, Suzi, and John Russell. *Pop Art Redefined*. London: Thames and Hudson, 1969.

Kostelanetz, Richard, ed. *The New American Arts*. New York: Horizon Press, circa 1965.

Lippard, Lucy. *Pop Art*. New York: Praeger, 1966.

Los Angeles County Museum of Art. *American Sculpture of the Sixties*. Los Angeles: Los Angeles County Museum of Art, 1968.

Mahsun, Carol Anne, ed. *Pop Art: The Critical Dialogue*. Ann Arbor: UMI Research Press, 1989.

Medina, José Ramon. *Marisol*. Caracas: Ediciones Armitano, 1968.

Moore College of Art. *Marisol*. Philadelphia: Moore College of Art, 1970.

Moritz, Charles, ed. *Current Biography*. New York: H. W. Wilson Co., 1968, pp. 241–44.

Museum Boymans-van Beuningen. *Marisol*. Rotterdam: Museum Boymans-van Beuningen, 1968.

Museum of Modern Art. *Americans 1963*. New York: Museum of Modern Art, 1963.

Nemser, Cindy. *Art Talk*. New York: Charles Scribner's Sons, 1975.

New York Cultural Center. *Marisol Prints, 1961–1973*. New York: New York Cultural Center, 1973.

Pierre, José. *An Illustrated Dictionary of Pop Art*. London: Eyre Methuen, 1975.

Rose, Barbara. *American Art Since 1900*. New York: Praeger, 1967.

Rubinstein, Charlotte Streifer. *American Women Artists*. New York: Aron, 1982.

Seitz, William. *The Art of Assemblage*. New York: Museum of Modern Art, 1961.

Worcester Art Museum. *Marisol*. Worcester, Mass.: Worcester Art Museum, 1971.

Periodicals and Newspapers

Amaya, Mario. "Face Sculptures." *Financial Times* (London), September 20, 1967.

"Americans 1963." *Art International* 7 (June 25, 1963): 71–75.

Amman, J. C. "Venedig: 34 Biennale." *Werk* 55 (August 1968): 566.

André, Michael. "Reviews and Previews: Marisol." *Art News* 72 (December 1973): 90.

———. "New York Reviews: Marisol." *Art News* 74 (May 1975): 94–95.

"Art." *Women's Wear Daily,* December 3, 1965, p. 32.

"Art: Collectors—A Life of Involvement." *Time* 91 (March 29, 1968): 68–75.

"Art: Sculpture—The Dollmaker." *Time* 85 (May 28, 1965): 80–81.

"Art and Artists." *New York Journal-American,* December 11, 1965.

"Art for Everyday Living: Painted Furs." *Art in America* 51 (October 1963): 97.

"Artists in Focus: Marisol." *American Artist* 50 (August 1986): 74.

Ashton, Dore. "New York Commentary: Acceleration in Discovery and Consumption—Marisol." *Studio International* 167 (May 1964): 214.

———. "New York Commentary: Historicism and Respect for Tradition—Marisol." *Studio International* 171 (June 1966): 278.

Ball, Ian. "Figures of State." *Daily Telegraph Magazine* (London), September 15, 1967, p. 20.

Barnitz, Jacqueline. "The Marisol Mask." *Artes Hispanicas* 1 (Autumn 1967): 35–49.

Baro, Gene. "A Gathering of Americans." *Arts* 37 (September 1963): 33.

Barrio-Garay, J. L. "El auge de la escultura en exposiciones individuales." *Goya* 115 (July 1973): 41.

Barry, Edward. "The Art of Marisol: Intriguing Objects Fashioned of Wood." *Chicago Tribune,* December 22, 1965, sec. 2, p. 9.

Berman, Avis. "A Bold and Incisive Way of Portraying Movers and Shakers." *Smithsonian* 14 (February 1984): 54–63.

Bernstein, Roberta. "Marisol as Portraitist: Artists and Artistes." *Arts* 55 (May 1981): 112–15.

———. "Marisol's Self-Portraits: The Dream and the Dreamer." *Arts* 59 (March 1985): 86–89.

Brett, Guy. "Some Younger Painters and Sculptors: The Wit of Marisol." *The Times* (London), September 25, 1967.

Brown, Gordon. "In the Galleries: Marisol." *Arts* 40 (June 1966): 45.

Browner, Millicent. "Sculptress, Own Model, Is 'A Beatnik' No Longer." *Indianapolis Star,* November 22, 1961.

Butler, J. T. "Worcester Art Museum Exhibition." *Connoisseur* 179 (January 1972): 59.

Butwin, David. "Statue Selectors Defend Choice." *Honolulu Advertiser,* March 15, 1967.

Calas, Nicolas. "Art Journal: Not Serious!" *Village Voice,* March 12, 1964, p. 8.

Campbell, Lawrence. "Marisol's Magic Mixtures." *Art News* 63 (March 1964): 38–41, 64–65.

———. "The Creative Eye of the Artist: Marisol." *Cosmopolitan* 156 (June 1964): 62–69.

Campos, Manuel. "Mesa de diseccion: Marisol triunfa en New York." *La Rivista* (Caracas), June 14, 1964, p. 5.

Canaday, John. "Toys by Artists Are Good Art and Good Toys." *New York Times*, December 22, 1963.

———. "Americans Once More." *New York Times*, May 20, 1964.

———. "Art: 15 Exhibit at the Modern." *New York Times*, May 22, 1964.

———. "Life Size Dolls on Display at Janis." *New York Times*, April 16, 1966.

Carroll, Karen. "Marisol." *School Arts* 86 (November 1986): 23.

Chapman, Daniel. "Marisol . . . A Brilliant Sculptress Shapes the Heads of State." *Look* 23 (November 14, 1967): 78–83.

Cicnerol, Florencio G. "Ronda de galerias." *Noticias de Arte* (April 1981): 8.

Coates, Robert M. "The Art Galleries: Extremes." *New Yorker* 16 (December 11, 1965): 219–22.

"Collectors: From Mondrian to Martial Airs." *Time* 91 (January 26, 1968): 56–61.

De Prenger, Kim. "On Understanding: The Artist as a Model." *School Arts* 85 (November 1985): 14.

Derfner, Phyllis. "New York: Marisol." *Art International* 19 (May 15, 1975): 67.

Edelman, Robert G. "Review of Exhibitions: Marisol at Sidney Janis." *Art in America* 72 (October 1984): 189.

"En Nueva York muestra de la escultura Venezolana Marisol represent del 'Pop Art.'" *La Esfera* (Caracas), March 4, 1964.

F.T.R. "Marisol." *Pictures on Exhibit* 31 (December 1967): 17.

Ferren, John. "Stable State of Mind." *Art News* 54 (May 1955): 22–23, 63–64.

"54–64 mostra a London." *Domus* 419 (October 1964): 54.

"Fifty-six Painters and Sculptors." *Art in America* 52 (August 1964): 76, 77.

Gardner, Paul. "Who Is Marisol?" *Art News* 88 (May 1989): 146–51.

Genauer, Emily. "57th St. and Environs: Marisol." *New York Herald Tribune*, April 16, 1966.

———. "On Art: Happy Hunting in a Cornucopia." *New York Herald Tribune*, November 25, 1967, p. 6.

Glueck, Grace. "It's Not Pop, It's Not Op It's Marisol." *New York Times Magazine*, March 7, 1965, pp. 34, 35, 45–49.

———. "A Marisol Sculpture Creates a Storm, and Loses, in Hawaii." *New York Times*, March 31, 1967.

———. "Marisol Shows Her Brooklyn Bridge Memorial." *New York Times*, April 16, 1988, p. 11.

Gold, Barbara. "Portrait of Marisol." *Interplay* 1 (January 1968): 52–55.

Goldberg, Jeff. "Pop Artist Marisol—20 Years After Her First Fame—Recalls Her Life and Loves," *People* 3 (March 24, 1975): 40–43.

Gosling, Nigel. "Gallery Guide." *The Observer* (London), September 24, 1967, p. 24.

Gray, Cleve. "Tatyana Grosman's Workshop." *Art in America* 53 (December 1965–January 1966): 85.

Grove, Nancy. "Marisol." *Art and Antiques* 6 (October 1989): 51.

Gruen, John. "Art: Marisol—Top to Bottom." *New York Herald Tribune*, March 8, 1964.

———. "Art: Op and Pop." *New York Herald Tribune*, December 12, 1965.

Haydon, Harold. "Art: Drawings: How They Reveal Artist's Power and Ambition." *Chicago Sunday Times*, January 2, 1966, p. 2.

Heinemann, Susan. "Reviews: Marisol." *Artforum* 13 (May 1975): 77.

Henry, Gerrit. "Reviews and Previews: Marisol." *Art News* 72 (Summer 1973): 92.

Hess, Thomas B. "The Phony Crisis in American Art." *Art News* 62 (Summer 1963): 24–28, 59–60.

————. "The Disrespectful Hand-maiden." *Art News* 63 (January 1965): 38–39, 57–58.

"How to Portray a Martyr?" *Time* 89 (May 12, 1967): 83.

James, Paula. "Making Aunt Sallys of the Royal Family." *Daily Mirror* (London), September 15, 1967, p. 9.

James, T., Jr. "Features: Marisol Escobar." *Women's Wear Daily*, February 25, 1964, p. 10.

"John Wayne, Who Rides Off Artfully in All Directions." *Life* 55 (December 20, 1963): 110–11.

Kimmelman, Michael. "Marisol." *New York Times*, May 19, 1989, p. 33.

Kingsley, April. "New York Letter: Marisol." *Art International* 17 (October 1973): 53.

————. "Sidney Janis Gallery Exhibition." *Burlington Magazine* 131 (July 1989): 508.

Kiplinger, Suzanne. "Art: Marisol at Stable." *Village Voice*, November 20, 1962, pp. 10, 32.

Kozloff, Max. "New York Letter: Marisol." *Art International* 6 (September 1962): 35.

Kuh, Katharine. "The Fine Arts: Notes of a Peripatetic Gallerygoer." *Saturday Review* 47 (April 25, 1964): 71.

"L'anima dannata della Pop Art." *Successo* (Milan), August 1964, pp. 17–18.

Larson, Kay. "Supper with Marisol." *New York Magazine* 17 (June 4, 1984): 70.

"Les grandes de ce monde dans le bois: reflets du monde." *L'Esprit* (Paris), September 19, 1967.

"A Letter from the Publisher." *Time* 89 (March 3, 1967): 4.

"Looks Like Men at Home." *Vogue*, November 16, 1966, p. 125.

Loring, John. "Marisol's Diptych: Impressions, Tracings, Hatchings." *Arts* 47 (April 1973): 69–70.

————. "Marisol Draws." *Arts* 49 (March 1975): 66–67.

Lynton, Norbert. "London Galleries." *Manchester Guardian*, September 25, 1967.

Marchiori, G. "La Biennale de Venise enlisée dans la lagure." *XX Siècle* n.s. 31 (December 1964): 134.

"Marisol." *American Artist* 50 (August 1988): 74.

"Marisol." *Time* 81 (June 7, 1963): 76–77.

"Marisol: Escultora Laconica." *El Nacional* (Caracas), September 3, 1966.

"Marisol at Stable." *New York Herald Tribune*, November 29, 1964.

"Marisol on Society." *New York Herald Tribune*, April 15, 1966.

"Marisol's Mannequins." *Horizon* 5 (March 1963): 102–4.

Mastai, M. L. D'Otrange. "New York News." *The Arts Review* 14 (July 14–28, 1962): 23.

Mayer, Phil. "Public Divided on Damien Model." *Honolulu Star Bulletin*, March 15, 1967.

Mellow, James R. "New York." *Art International* 11 (November 1967): 59.

————. "New York Letter." *Art International* 12 (January 1968): 64.

Metken, G. "Documenta." *Deutsche Bauzeitung* 102 (October 1968): 795.

Michals, Duane. "The Fashion Independent: Marisol." *Harper's Bazaar,* October 1963, pp. 198–201.

Neu, Renée S. "The Artist as Jeweler." *Art in America* 55 (November–December 1967): 76–77.

"The New Whitney." *Newsweek* 68 (October 3, 1966): 101–3.

"New York: exposition des sculptures dans Central Park." *Architecture d'Aujourd'hui* 39 (December 1967): lv.

Nigroan, L. "Worcester Art Museum, Massachusetts, Exhibition." *Craft Horizons* 31 (December 1971): 50–51.

O'Doherty, Brian. "Marisol: The Enigma of the Self-Image." *New York Times,* March 1, 1964, p. 23.

Oeri, G. "Marisol." *Quadrum* 16 (1964): 148–49.

Perrault, John. "The Identity Behind Marisol's Face." *Village Voice,* May 17, 1973, pp. 46–47.

Phillips, Deborah C. "New York Reviews: Marisol." *Art News* 80 (September 1981): 231.

Picard, Lil. "Wo Wilde Avantgarde Gefordert Wird." *Die-Welt* 84 (August 9, 1962): 9.

————. "Kritik, Protest und Neue Ideen." *Die-Welt* 86 (March 28, 1964).

————. "Voyeu Rama." *East Village Other,* April 1966, p. 11.

Piene, Nan R. "New York: Gallery Notes." *Art in America* 54 (March–April 1966): 128.

"Portrait." *Art News Annual* 28 (1959): 29.

"Portrait." *Künstwerk* 19 (April 1966): 29.

"Pourtant, c'est un témoignage d'admiration." *Paris-Presse,* September 16, 1967.

Raynor, Vivien. "In the Galleries: Marisol." *Arts* 35 (May–June 1961): 94.

————. "In the Galleries: Marisol." *Arts* 36 (September 1962): 44–45.

————. "Art: Marisol Sculpture from Leonardo Painting." *New York Times,* June 1, 1984.

"Reviews and Previews: Marisol." *Art News* 56 (November 1957): 14.

"Reviews and Previews: Marisol." *Art News* 60 (April 1961): 10.

"Reviews and Previews: Marisol." *Art News* 61 (May 1962): 10.

"Reviews and Previews: Marisol." *Art News* 65 (Summer 1966): 13.

"Reviews and Previews: Marisol." *Art News* 66 (November 1967): 60.

"Reviews and Previews: New York Painters' and Sculptors' Drawings." *Art News* 56 (January 1958): 19.

Rewald, Alice. "Le petit monde de Marisol." *Gazette de Lausanne,* p. 19.

Roberts, C. "New York." *Aujourd'hui* 7 (May 1963): 48.

————. "Lettre de New York." *Aujourd'hui* 8 (October 1963): 201.

Rosenberg, Harold. "From Pollock to Pop: Twenty Years of Painting and Sculpture." *Holiday* 39 (March 1966): 96–104.

Sandler, Irving. "In the Art Galleries." *New York Post,* May 20, 1962, p. 10.

"Sculpture in Wood of Royal Family Shown." *Daily Telegraph* (London), September 15, 1967.

Shaw-Eagle, Joanna. "American Women in Sculpture." *Harper's Bazaar,* August 1981, p. 163.

Sheppard, Eugenia. "Inside Fashion: She Likes Parties." *New York Herald Tribune,* April 19, 1966.

"Sidney Janis Gallery Exhibition." *Craft Horizons* 33 (August 1973): 29.

"Sidney Janis Gallery Exhibition." *Craft Horizons* 35 (August 1975): 44.

Silverthome, Jeanne. "Reviews: Marisol." *Artforum* 28 (October 1984): 90.

Simon, Joan. "Chers maîtres." *Art in America* 69 (October 1981): 120–21.

Slesin, Suzanne. "The New York Artist in Residence." *Art News* 77 (November 1978): 74.

Steinem, Gloria. "Marisol: The Face Behind the Mask." *Glamour* 51 (June 1964): 92–97, 127.

Tallmer, Jerry. "Whimsy Worth Crowing About." *New York Post,* April 28, 1989.

"The Third Dimension." *Newsweek* (May 8, 1967): 99.

Tillim, Sidney. "In the Galleries: Marisol." *Arts* 38 (April 1964): 28–29.

Vergani, Leonardo. "Una scultricia transforma i personaggi in sarcofaghi." *Corriere della Sera* (Milan), September 22, 1967, p. 3.

Wasserman, Edith. "Remember Dada? Today We Call Him Pop." *Art Education* 19 (May 1966): 12–17.

Westfall, Stephen. "Arts Reviews: Marisol." *Arts* 55 (June 1981): 26.

———. "Arts Reviews: Marisol." *Arts* 59 (November 1984): 38–39.

Willard, Charlotte. "In the Art Galleries." *New York Post,* December 12, 1965, p. 47.

———. "Eye to I." *Art in America* 54 (March–April 1966): 52.

Williams, Michaela. "Mum Marisol." *Chicago Daily News,* December 15, 1965.

Wolff, Theodore F. "From Fun and Games to Moving Statement." *Christian Science Monitor,* March 30, 1987.

"Wood Carvers' Comeback: Young U.S. Sculptors Revive Neglected Art." *Life* 16 (July 14, 1958): 54–57, 59–60.

"Young Talent USA." *Art in America* 51 (June 1962): 50.

Index

Photography credits

Rudolph Burckhardt: pp. 11, 13, 14, 16
Geoffrey Clements: pp. 27, 65, 69
Allan Finkelman: pp. 31, 32, 33, 35, 38, 77, 83
Joseph Klima, Jr.: p. 53
Thomas Loonan: pp. 19, 23
Otto E. Nelson: pp. 29, 34, 73, 79
Jeffery Nintzel: p. 71
John D. Schiff: p. 18
Joseph Szaszfai: p. 24
Michael Tropea: p. 49
Malcolm Varon: p. 81
Rolland White: pp. 57, 59, 63, 75

Photographs courtesy of the artist: pp. 13, 14, 16, 18
Photograph courtesy of the Leo Castelli Gallery Photo Archives: p. 11
Photographs courtesy of the Sidney Janis Gallery, New York City: pp. 27, 29, 31, 32, 33, 34, 35, 36, 38, 40, 65, 69, 73 *Green Fish,* 77, 79

**Magical Mixtures:
Marisol Portrait Sculpture**
was edited by Frances K. Stevenson and Dru Dowdy, in the National Portrait Gallery Publications Office; designed in the office of George Sexton Associates, Washington, D.C.; electronically typeset in Adobe Gill Sans by Unicom Graphics, Washington, D.C.; and printed in four colors on 80 lb. Centura Gloss by Schneidereith and Sons, Inc., Baltimore, Maryland.